POWER QUERY for POWER BI and EXCEL

Transform and Shape Data

Kiet Huynh

Table of Contents

CHAPTER I
Introduction to Power Query

Part 1. Getting Started with Power Query

1.1 What is Power Query?

In the world of data analysis and business intelligence, the ability to extract, transform, and load (ETL) data is of paramount importance. Data often resides in various sources, such as databases, spreadsheets, web services, and text files, and it comes in different formats and structures. To make this data usable for analysis and reporting, it needs to be cleaned, transformed, and combined effectively. This is where Power Query steps in as an indispensable tool in the Microsoft ecosystem, offering a comprehensive solution for data wrangling.

Understanding the Essence of Power Query

Power Query is an integral part of Microsoft Power BI and Excel, designed to address the complexities of data preparation, making it accessible to a broad audience, from data analysts to business users. It provides a user-friendly, intuitive, and highly capable interface for data extraction, transformation, and loading.

Data Extraction

Power Query empowers users to connect to various data sources with ease. Whether your data is stored in a local Excel file, a remote SQL database, or an online source like SharePoint or a web service, Power Query allows you to establish these connections effortlessly. With just a few clicks, you can import the data you need directly into your Power BI or Excel environment.

Example: Imagine you have an Excel file containing sales data, and you want to merge it with your SQL database's customer data to create a comprehensive sales report. Power Query enables you to establish connections to both data sources and bring them together.

Data Transformation

Once the data is loaded, it often requires extensive transformations. Raw data is rarely ready for analysis, and it typically contains inconsistencies, missing values, or irrelevant information. Power Query provides an array of transformation options to help you clean and shape your data.

Example: Suppose your sales data contains a column of dates in different formats (e.g., "01/05/2023" and "January 5, 2023"). Power Query can standardize these dates into a consistent format for analysis.

Data Enrichment

Power Query can also enhance your data by merging it with other datasets or adding calculated columns. This feature allows you to derive additional insights and context from your information.

Example: You might want to enrich your sales data with external data, such as population statistics for the regions where you operate. Power Query can merge this external dataset with your sales data, providing valuable context for your analysis.

Data Combination

It is common to work with multiple data sources or tables that need to be combined to create comprehensive datasets. Power Query simplifies this process, enabling you to merge, append, or join tables seamlessly.

Example: Combining data from sales, marketing, and customer support departments to create a holistic view of customer interactions. Power Query can merge these disparate datasets into a single, cohesive report.

Benefits of Using Power Query

The capabilities of Power Query extend beyond its user-friendly interface. It offers numerous benefits that make it an indispensable tool for data professionals:

1. Efficiency

Power Query automates data transformation tasks, reducing manual efforts and the risk of errors. You can create repeatable workflows that ensure consistent and accurate data preparation.

2. Flexibility

It is highly adaptable and can handle a wide variety of data sources and formats. Whether you're working with structured data, unstructured data, or semi-structured data, Power Query can handle it all.

3. Reusability

Power Query allows you to create queries that can be reused across different projects. This reusability simplifies data preparation for recurring analyses.

4. Integration

Seamless integration with Microsoft Excel and Power BI means that you can incorporate Power Query into your existing workflow, enhancing your data analysis capabilities.

Power Query in Action

Let's walk through a practical example to illustrate the power and versatility of Power Query.

Scenario: You are a data analyst tasked with preparing data for a sales report. The data comes from multiple sources, including an Excel file with order information, a SQL database with customer data, and a web service with product details.

Step 1: Data Extraction

With Power Query, you connect to these diverse data sources effortlessly. You import the Excel file, establish a connection to the SQL database, and retrieve data from the web service, all from within your Power BI or Excel environment.

Step 2: Data Transformation

The data from these sources may have inconsistencies. For instance, the product names from the web service have special characters that need to be removed, and the dates in the Excel file have varying formats. Power Query enables you to clean and standardize this data with ease.

Step 3: Data Enrichment

You decide to add more context to the data by incorporating external information. You merge the customer data from the SQL database with your sales data, allowing you to analyze the relationship between customer demographics and sales.

Step 4: Data Combination

Lastly, you append the product details from the web service to your sales data, creating a comprehensive dataset for your report.

This practical example demonstrates how Power Query simplifies the complex process of data preparation. It allows you to efficiently extract, transform, enrich, and combine data from various sources, ultimately enabling you to derive valuable insights for your business.

Conclusion

Power Query is a game-changing tool that empowers individuals and organizations to harness the full potential of their data. Its ability to extract, transform, and load data efficiently and accurately makes it a valuable asset in the world of data analysis. With Power Query, data professionals can focus on deriving insights and making informed decisions rather than struggling with data preparation.

In the subsequent chapters of this book, we will delve deeper into the features and functionalities of Power Query, exploring its various capabilities and applications. By the end of this journey, you will have a comprehensive understanding of how to leverage Power Query to transform and shape data for your specific needs in Power BI and Excel.

1.2 Power Query in Power BI and Excel

In the ever-evolving landscape of data analytics and business intelligence, the ability to harness and mold data into valuable insights is a crucial component. Power BI and Microsoft Excel are two of the most popular tools in this arena, and they owe much of their data transformation capabilities to Power Query. In this section, we will delve deep into how Power Query is integrated into both Power BI and Excel, highlighting its significance and versatility in both environments.

The Power Query Integration

Power Query was initially developed as a standalone tool, but it quickly found its way into Microsoft's suite of business intelligence and data analysis tools. It's now seamlessly integrated into both Power BI and Excel, and this integration is a game-changer for anyone working with data. It brings power, flexibility, and efficiency to the process of data transformation and preparation.

Power Query in Power BI

Example: Imagine you are a data analyst at a retail company, and you have sales data stored in a Power BI dataset. This dataset is updated regularly with new sales information. Power Query in Power BI allows you to connect to this dataset, extract the data, and perform transformations to ensure the data is clean and ready for analysis. With scheduled refreshes, your reports stay up to date automatically.

Power Query in Excel

Example: Now, consider you are a financial analyst working with Excel. You have a complex financial model with data from multiple sources, including spreadsheets and external databases. Power Query in Excel allows you to establish connections to these sources, pull the data into Excel, and apply transformations directly within your Excel workbook. This means you can work with fresh, accurate data without leaving the familiar Excel environment.

1. Data Transformation within the Tool

Power Query brings data transformation capabilities directly into your analysis tools. Whether you are creating reports and dashboards in Power BI or building complex financial models in Excel, you don't need to switch to another tool for data preparation. This streamlines your workflow and saves time.

2. User-Friendly Interface

Both Power BI and Excel have integrated Power Query with user-friendly interfaces. This means that data professionals, business analysts, and even non-technical users can harness the power of Power Query without extensive coding or scripting. The visual interface simplifies the data preparation process.

3. Data Refresh and Automation

Power Query in both Power BI and Excel allows you to schedule data refreshes. This means your data is always up to date without manual intervention. For example, in Power BI, you can set up dataflows that automatically refresh the data, ensuring your reports reflect the latest information. In Excel, you can create queries and refresh them with a single click.

4. Seamless Collaboration

In a business environment, collaboration is essential. Power Query in Power BI and Excel allows multiple users to work with the same data sources and queries. This ensures consistency in data preparation and reporting across teams.

Example: You're part of a data analysis team at a multinational corporation. Different team members are responsible for different aspects of the analysis. With Power Query in Power BI, you can create dataflows, and your colleagues can access and use these dataflows in their reports, ensuring everyone works with the same clean and transformed data.

Power Query in Action

To truly appreciate the power of Power Query within Power BI and Excel, let's explore two real-world scenarios:

Scenario 1: Power Query in Power BI

You are a data analyst at a retail company, and you use Power BI to create monthly sales reports. Your sales data is stored in a SQL Server database, and you need to merge it with data from an Excel spreadsheet that contains promotional campaign information. Here's how Power Query in Power BI makes it possible:

1. Data Extraction: In Power BI, you connect to your SQL Server database and the Excel spreadsheet as data sources. You create queries for each source, and Power Query pulls the data into Power BI.

2. Data Transformation: The dates in your SQL database are in a different format than the dates in the Excel spreadsheet. Power Query enables you to standardize the date format so that you can combine the data accurately.

3. Data Combination: You use Power Query to merge the two datasets based on a common product ID. This results in a single dataset that combines sales data with campaign information, providing valuable insights into the impact of promotional campaigns on sales.

Scenario 2: Power Query in Excel

You are a financial analyst working with an extensive Excel financial model that requires data from multiple sources, including a SharePoint list, an SQL database, and a series of CSV files. Here's how Power Query in Excel streamlines your workflow:

1. Data Extraction: In Excel, you create separate queries for each data source, including the SharePoint list, the SQL database, and the CSV files. Power Query extracts the data from these sources and brings it into your Excel workbook.

2. Data Transformation: The SharePoint list contains additional columns that are not relevant to your analysis. With Power Query, you remove these columns to simplify your data.

3. Data Combination: Power Query allows you to combine data from the SQL database, CSV files, and SharePoint list into a single worksheet within Excel. This consolidated dataset is used as the basis for your financial model.

These scenarios demonstrate the flexibility and utility of Power Query in both Power BI and Excel. Whether you are working on data visualization in Power BI or complex financial modeling in Excel, Power Query enhances your capabilities by enabling data extraction, transformation, and combination directly within the tools you use.

Conclusion

Power Query is more than just a data transformation tool; it's a catalyst for unlocking the full potential of your data analysis and reporting efforts. The seamless integration of Power Query within Power BI and Excel simplifies the often complex process of data preparation, making it accessible to a wide range of users. With Power Query at your disposal, you can focus on what matters most—gaining insights from your data and making informed decisions.

As you progress through this book, you'll explore the depth and breadth of Power Query's features and functionalities, empowering you to shape and transform data effectively within the environments of Power BI and Excel.

1.3 Installation and Setup

To harness the capabilities of Power Query in Power BI and Excel, the first step is to ensure that you have it installed and properly set up. This chapter will guide you through the installation process, regardless of whether you're using Power BI or Excel. We'll cover the requirements, provide step-by-step instructions, and address potential challenges you might encounter. By the end of this chapter, you'll be well-prepared to embark on your data transformation journey using Power Query.

 Requirements

Before we dive into the installation process, let's ensure you have all the prerequisites in place.

For Power BI

1. Power BI Desktop: To use Power Query within Power BI, you'll need to have Power BI Desktop installed on your computer. This is a free application that can be downloaded from the official Power BI website.

2. Access to Data Sources: Make sure you have access to the data sources you intend to connect to. These sources can be databases, online services, local files, or web data.

For Excel

1. Microsoft Excel: You'll need a version of Microsoft Excel that supports Power Query. Power Query is available in Excel 2010, Excel 2013, Excel 2016, Excel 2019, and Excel for Microsoft 365. Ensure you have one of these Excel versions installed.

2. Office 365 Subscription: If you're using Excel for Microsoft 365, you'll need an Office 365 subscription. Power Query is often available as part of the Office 365 package.

3. Access to Data Sources: Just like in Power BI, you should have access to the data sources you plan to connect to.

 Installation Steps

For Power BI

Step 1: Download Power BI Desktop

- Go to the official Power BI website (https://powerbi.microsoft.com/).

- Navigate to the "Downloads" section.

- Click on the "Power BI Desktop" download link.

- Follow the on-screen instructions to download the installer.

Step 2: Install Power BI Desktop

- Locate the downloaded installer and run it.

- Follow the installation wizard's steps to complete the installation.

- Once the installation is complete, you will have Power BI Desktop on your computer.

Example: You are a data analyst interested in using Power Query in Power BI. You visit the Power BI website, download the Power BI Desktop installer, and install it on your Windows computer. Now you're ready to start using Power Query.

For Excel

Step 1: Open Excel

- Launch Microsoft Excel. Ensure you are using a compatible version of Excel (2010, 2013, 2016, 2019, or Excel for Microsoft 365).

Step 2: Load Power Query Add-In

- In Excel, click on the "Data" tab in the ribbon.

- Look for the "Get & Transform Data" group.

- If you don't see it, you might need to enable the Power Query add-in. To do this, click "File," then "Options," and navigate to the "Add-Ins" section.

- In the "Add-Ins" window, select "COM Add-ins" from the dropdown and click "Go."

- Check the "Microsoft Office Power Query for Excel" box and click "OK."

Step 3: Access Power Query

- After enabling the add-in, you should now see the "Get Data" button in the "Data" tab. Click on it to access Power Query.

Example: You are an accountant using Microsoft Excel 2016. To use Power Query, you open Excel, enable the Power Query add-in, and access it through the "Get Data" button in the "Data" tab.

Potential Challenges and Solutions

During installation and setup, you might encounter some common challenges. Let's address a few of them:

Challenge 1: Add-In Not Available

If you're using Excel, you might not see the "Get & Transform Data" group in the "Data" tab. This is because the Power Query add-in is not enabled by default.

Solution: Follow the steps outlined in the installation process to enable the Power Query add-in.

Challenge 2: Data Source Connection Issues

You might encounter difficulties connecting to specific data sources, especially if they require specific drivers or credentials.

Solution: Ensure you have the necessary drivers installed for your data sources. Double-check your credentials and make sure you have the required permissions to access the data.

Challenge 3: Software Version Compatibility

If you're using an older version of Excel, Power Query might not be available or as feature-rich as in newer versions.

Solution: Consider upgrading to a more recent version of Excel to access the full suite of Power Query features.

Challenge 4: Internet Access and Updates

Power BI Desktop and Office 365 may require internet access for updates and licensing verification.

Solution: Ensure that your computer has internet access during installation and periodically for updates.

Conclusion

Installing and setting up Power Query is the foundation of your data transformation journey in Power BI and Excel. With the right software and add-ins in place, you are well on your way to leveraging the power and flexibility of Power Query for data extraction, transformation, and loading.

As you progress through this book, you will learn how to put these tools to work, from connecting to data sources to performing complex data transformations with ease. Your understanding of the installation process ensures that you have a solid start on your path to becoming a proficient user of Power Query.

Part 2. Data Sources and Connections

2.1 Connecting to Various Data Sources

Welcome Chapter 2: Data Sources and Connections

2.1 Connecting to Various Data Sources

In this chapter, we will delve into the essential aspects of connecting to a variety of data sources using Power Query. The ability to connect to data sources is the first step in transforming and shaping data for your Power BI and Excel projects. With Power Query, you can seamlessly link to different data repositories, databases, files, and online services. This chapter will equip you with the knowledge and practical skills needed to access your data efficiently and effectively.

Understanding Data Sources:

Data sources can come in various forms, and Power Query is designed to work with a wide range of them. Before we dive into the specifics of connecting, let's explore the types of data sources you may encounter:

1. Databases: This includes database management systems like Microsoft SQL Server, MySQL, Oracle, and more. Power Query enables you to extract data from these systems, making it useful for business intelligence and reporting.

2. Files: Power Query can connect to various file formats such as Excel workbooks, CSV files, XML, JSON, and even text files. This versatility ensures you can work with data stored in files from different applications and platforms.

3. Web Data Sources: You can extract data from websites and web services, which is especially useful for web scraping, analytics, and monitoring. Common web data sources include REST APIs, HTML tables, and JSON responses.

4. Online Services: Many cloud-based platforms and services offer APIs for data extraction. Power Query supports connections to platforms like Azure Data Lake Storage, SharePoint Online, and more.

Connecting to Data Sources:

Now, let's get into the practical aspect of connecting to various data sources:

1. Connecting to Databases: When connecting to databases, you'll need to provide connection details such as server addresses, authentication credentials, and database selection. For instance, to connect to a Microsoft SQL Server database, you'll specify the server address, database name, and your authentication method (e.g., Windows, SQL Server, or Azure Active Directory).

2. Importing Data from Files: Importing data from files is straightforward. For Excel files, you can specify the file path and choose specific worksheets or tables. When working with CSV files, you'll define the file's location and delimiter (e.g., comma or semicolon).

3. Web Data Sources: To connect to web data sources, you'll typically provide a URL or endpoint. You may need to include additional parameters like API keys or query strings to access specific data. For example, when connecting to a REST API, you'll input the API endpoint and any required headers or query parameters.

4. Online Services: Connecting to online services often involves authentication and authorization steps. You'll need to provide credentials and potentially generate API keys or access tokens. For services like SharePoint Online, you may need to specify the site URL and authentication method.

Illustrative Examples:

Let's illustrate these concepts with some examples:

Example 1 - Connecting to a SQL Database:

Suppose you want to connect to a Microsoft SQL Server database that hosts sales data. You would provide the following information:

- Server Address: sqlserver.example.com

- Database Name: SalesDB

- Authentication: SQL Server Authentication (Username and Password)

Example 2 - Importing Data from an Excel File:

If you have an Excel workbook with sales data, you can connect to it by specifying:

- File Path: C:\Path\to\salesdata.xlsx

- Worksheet: SalesDataSheet

Example 3 - Accessing a REST API:

To retrieve weather data from a weather service's REST API, you'd input:

- API Endpoint: https://api.weather.example.com

- Headers: API Key: YourAPIKey

- Query Parameters: Location: CityName, Date: Today

Conclusion:

Connecting to various data sources using Power Query is the foundation of data transformation and shaping in Power BI and Excel. Understanding the types of data sources and how to connect to them is pivotal for successful data analysis and reporting. This chapter will equip you with the knowledge and skills to harness the power of Power Query for your data-driven projects.

2.2 Importing Data from Databases

In this section, we will explore the intricacies of importing data from databases using Power Query. Databases are a rich source of structured information, and the ability to efficiently extract and transform this data is crucial for data analysis and reporting in both Power BI and Excel. This chapter will provide you with a comprehensive understanding of how to import data from various types of databases, be it a relational database like Microsoft SQL Server, an open-source database like MySQL, or other data storage systems.

Understanding Database Connections:

Databases serve as repositories for a wide range of data, from customer records and product catalogs to financial transactions and more. Power Query enables you to connect to databases using various connectors, allowing you to access and import data tables, views, or stored procedures. Before we dive into the practical aspects of importing data, let's explore the components of database connections:

1. Connection Details: When connecting to a database, you must provide essential information, including the server address, database name, and authentication method. For instance, connecting to a Microsoft SQL Server database requires specifying the server's address, the target database, and your authentication credentials, which may include a username and password or integrated Windows authentication.

2. Query Language: Power Query utilizes database-specific query languages to interact with the database. For example, when connecting to SQL Server, it employs Transact-SQL (T-SQL) for querying, while MySQL connections rely on Structured Query Language (SQL). You'll use these languages to extract and transform data.

Importing Data from Databases:

Now, let's delve into the practical steps involved in importing data from databases:

1. Connecting to the Database: Launch Power Query within Power BI or Excel, and initiate a new connection to the database. Provide the necessary connection details, including the server address and authentication credentials.

2. Selecting Data: After establishing the connection, you'll be presented with a navigator that displays the available tables, views, and stored procedures within the database. Select the specific data source you want to import.

3. Query Editor: Once you've chosen the data source, the Query Editor window opens. Here, you can perform various data transformations and filter out irrelevant data before loading it into your Power BI or Excel workbook. You can apply filters, remove columns, rename columns, and more.

4. Load Data: After you've prepared the data to your satisfaction, load it into your Power BI report or Excel spreadsheet. You can choose to load it directly or create a connection-only query, which allows for data transformation in subsequent steps.

Illustrative Examples:

Let's illustrate the process with two examples, one for Microsoft SQL Server and another for MySQL:

Example 1 - Importing Data from a Microsoft SQL Server Database:

Suppose you have a Microsoft SQL Server database that contains sales data. Here's how you would import it using Power Query:

1. Provide the server address, e.g., sqlserver.example.com.

2. Specify the database name, e.g., SalesDB.

3. Choose the data source, such as the "SalesData" table.

4. In the Query Editor, you can perform actions like filtering by date, removing unnecessary columns, and renaming columns.

Example 2 - Importing Data from a MySQL Database:

For a MySQL database with customer information, the process would be similar:

1. Enter the server address, e.g., mysql.example.com.

2. Indicate the database name, e.g., CustomerDB.

3. Select the "Customers" table or view.

4. In the Query Editor, you can perform transformations like converting date formats and aggregating data.

Conclusion:

Importing data from databases is a fundamental skill for data professionals, and Power Query simplifies the process by providing a user-friendly interface for connecting to and transforming data from a variety of database systems. This chapter has equipped you with the knowledge and practical skills needed to import data from databases, helping you harness the power of Power Query for your data analysis and reporting tasks.

2.3 Working with Files: Excel, CSV, and more

In this section, we'll dive into the comprehensive process of working with files, including Excel spreadsheets, CSV files, and various other file formats, using Power Query. Files are a common source of data for many analysts and organizations. Power Query simplifies the task of extracting, transforming, and loading data from files into Power BI and Excel, enabling data professionals to efficiently manage, analyze, and visualize information.

Understanding File Sources:

Files can store a wide range of data, from financial reports in Excel to log data in CSV format and even structured data in formats like XML and JSON. Before we delve into the specifics of working with files, let's explore the types of file sources you may encounter:

1. Excel Files: Excel workbooks are widely used for data storage. Power Query allows you to connect to Excel files, worksheets, and tables within those workbooks. You can also consolidate data from multiple Excel files.

2. CSV Files: Comma-separated values (CSV) files are a standard format for tabular data. Power Query supports connecting to CSV files, where you can specify delimiters and perform data transformations.

3. Other File Formats: Power Query is versatile and can connect to various file formats, including XML, JSON, text files, and more. You can adapt your query to handle the specific structure of these files.

Working with Files:

Now, let's explore the practical aspects of working with files:

1. Connecting to Files: To initiate a connection to a file, open Power Query within Power BI or Excel. Select the desired file source (e.g., Excel, CSV, XML) and provide the file path. For Excel files, you can choose specific worksheets or named tables. For CSV files, you can define the delimiter used.

2. Query Editor: Once you've connected to a file, the Query Editor interface opens, displaying the data from the file. Here, you can perform data transformations, such as filtering rows, renaming columns, changing data types, and merging tables.

3. Data Transformation: Depending on your data's structure, you can apply transformations like pivoting columns, unpivoting data, and merging queries. These operations are essential for preparing data for analysis and visualization.

4. Load Data: After applying the necessary transformations, you can load the data into your Power BI report or Excel workbook. You can choose to load it directly into a worksheet or data model or create a connection-only query for further data shaping.

Illustrative Examples:

Let's illustrate the process with two examples, one for working with an Excel file and another for a CSV file:

Example 1 - Working with an Excel File:

Suppose you have an Excel workbook named "SalesData.xlsx" with multiple worksheets. You want to import data from the "Sales" worksheet:

1. Provide the file path: C:\Path\to\SalesData.xlsx.

2. Choose the "Sales" worksheet.

3. In the Query Editor, you can perform actions like filtering by date, renaming columns, and changing data types.

Example 2 - Working with a CSV File:

For a CSV file containing customer information, the process would be as follows:

1. Enter the file path: C:\Path\to\CustomerData.csv.

2. Specify the delimiter used, such as a comma or semicolon.

3. In the Query Editor, you can perform transformations like removing duplicate rows and pivoting columns.

Conclusion:

Working with files, including Excel spreadsheets, CSV files, and other formats, is a fundamental aspect of data analysis. Power Query simplifies the process by providing a user-friendly interface for connecting to files and performing data transformations. This chapter equips you with the knowledge and skills necessary to work with files efficiently, helping you make the most of Power Query in your data-driven projects.

2.4 Web Data Sources

In this section, we will explore the process of connecting to web data sources using Power Query. The web is a vast repository of information, and Power Query enables you to extract and transform data from websites and web services for use in Power BI and Excel. Whether you need to gather data for analysis, reporting, or monitoring, this chapter will provide a comprehensive guide on how to connect to web data sources effectively.

Understanding Web Data Sources:

Web data sources encompass a wide array of data available on the internet, including structured data from websites, JSON or XML data from APIs, HTML tables, and more. Before we dive into the practical aspects of connecting to web data sources, let's explore the types of web data sources you may encounter:

1. REST APIs: Many web services and platforms offer RESTful APIs for data retrieval. Power Query can connect to these APIs, allowing you to request specific data by providing API endpoints and parameters.

2. HTML Tables: You can extract data from HTML tables on web pages. This is useful for web scraping and extracting tabular data from websites.

3. JSON and XML Data: Web APIs often return data in JSON or XML format. Power Query can parse and transform these data formats into structured tables for analysis.

4. Web Services: Online services like weather forecasts, financial market data, and social media feeds offer APIs for data access. Power Query can connect to these services by providing API keys or authentication details.

Connecting to Web Data Sources:

Now, let's explore the practical steps involved in connecting to web data sources:

1. Identify the Data Source: Begin by identifying the web data source you want to connect to. This could be a specific website, a REST API, or an online service. You'll need to determine the source's URL or API endpoint.

2. Authentication and Authorization: For secured web data sources, you may need to provide authentication credentials or API keys. Power Query allows you to input these details securely.

3. Request Data: Once you've identified the data source and, if necessary, provided authentication details, you can create a request to retrieve data. This might involve specifying query parameters to filter or refine the data.

4. Data Transformation: After retrieving data, it often requires transformation to fit your needs. You can perform actions like filtering rows, renaming columns, and changing data types in the Query Editor.

5. Load Data: Finally, you can load the transformed data into your Power BI report or Excel workbook, where you can use it for analysis and reporting.

Illustrative Examples:

Let's illustrate the process with two examples, one for connecting to a REST API and another for extracting data from an HTML table:

Example 1 - Connecting to a REST API:

Suppose you want to gather weather data from a weather service's REST API. Here's how you would do it using Power Query:

1. Provide the API endpoint: https://api.weather.example.com.

2. If required, input authentication details or API keys.

3. Specify query parameters, such as the location (CityName) and date (Today).

4. In the Query Editor, you can further transform the data, perhaps by filtering out unnecessary information or renaming columns.

Example 2 - Extracting Data from an HTML Table:

If you want to scrape data from a website's HTML table, follow these steps:

1. Enter the URL of the web page containing the table.

2. Power Query will fetch the HTML data from the page.

3. Use the Query Editor to locate the table in the HTML structure and transform the data into a structured table.

Conclusion:

Connecting to web data sources using Power Query is a valuable skill for data professionals and analysts. The ability to access data from REST APIs, web pages, and online services opens up a world of possibilities for data analysis and reporting. This chapter has equipped you with the knowledge and practical skills needed to connect to web data sources effectively, allowing you to harness the power of Power Query for your data-driven projects.

2.5 Importing Data from Online Services

In this section, we will delve into the process of importing data from online services using Power Query. Online services, including cloud-based platforms and web applications, offer APIs and data access points for retrieving information. Power Query facilitates the seamless integration of data from online services into Power BI and Excel, enabling data professionals to access and utilize a wealth of online data for analysis, reporting, and decision-making.

Understanding Online Services:

Online services encompass a wide spectrum of cloud-based platforms and web applications that provide data access through APIs. These services can include everything from cloud storage to social media platforms, marketing analytics tools, and more. Before we explore the practical aspects of connecting to online services, it's important to understand the types of online services you may encounter:

1. Cloud Storage Services: Platforms like Azure Data Lake Storage, Google Drive, and Dropbox offer APIs for accessing and importing files and data from cloud storage.

2. Social Media APIs: Social media platforms like Facebook, Twitter, and Instagram provide APIs to retrieve data such as posts, comments, and user information.

3. Marketing and Analytics Platforms: Tools like Google Analytics, HubSpot, and Salesforce offer APIs for extracting marketing data, sales information, and website analytics.

4. Online Business Tools: Applications like Microsoft SharePoint Online, Salesforce, and Slack provide data access points to retrieve information stored in these online tools.

Importing Data from Online Services:

Now, let's explore the practical steps involved in importing data from online services:

1. Identification and Authentication: To begin, you'll need to identify the online service you wish to connect to. If required, provide authentication credentials, API keys, or access tokens to access the service securely.

2. Select Data Source: Determine the specific data source or resource you want to import. This could be a dataset, a specific folder in cloud storage, a social media feed, or other resources provided by the online service's API.

3. API Endpoint and Parameters: If the online service offers multiple endpoints or data filtering options, specify the API endpoint and any necessary parameters to target the data you need.

4. Data Transformation: After retrieving data, you may need to transform it in the Query Editor. This might involve filtering, renaming columns, changing data types, and aggregating data to meet your analysis requirements.

5. Load Data: Once you've prepared the data, load it into your Power BI report or Excel workbook for analysis, visualization, and reporting.

Illustrative Examples:

Let's illustrate the process with two examples, one for connecting to a cloud storage service and another for retrieving data from a social media platform:

Example 1 - Importing Data from Azure Data Lake Storage:

Suppose you need to retrieve sales data stored in Azure Data Lake Storage. Here's how you would do it using Power Query:

1. Provide authentication details, including your Azure Active Directory (AAD) credentials.

2. Specify the API endpoint for the sales data file within the storage.

3. In the Query Editor, you can further transform the data, such as renaming columns or filtering by date.

Example 2 - Retrieving Social Media Posts from Twitter:

For gathering social media posts from Twitter, the process would be as follows:

1. Input your Twitter API key and access token for authentication.

2. Define the Twitter API endpoint for retrieving posts.

3. Specify query parameters like the user's Twitter handle and date range.

4. In the Query Editor, you can perform transformations like sentiment analysis on the text of the tweets.

Conclusion:

Importing data from online services is a valuable skill for data professionals, as it opens up access to a wealth of data sources in the cloud and on the web. The ability to connect to online services and retrieve data for analysis and reporting is a key feature of Power Query. This chapter has equipped you with the knowledge and practical skills needed to import data from online services effectively, enabling you to harness the power of Power Query for your data-driven projects.

Part 3. Data Loading and Transformations

3.1 Loading Data into Power Query

In this section, we will explore the fundamental process of loading data into Power Query. Data loading is the first critical step in the data transformation and shaping journey within Power BI and Excel. This chapter will provide a detailed guide on how to load data from various sources into Power Query, enabling you to start your data transformation and analysis effectively.

Understanding Data Loading:

Loading data into Power Query is the initial phase of the data transformation process. It involves the retrieval of data from external sources such as databases, files, web services, and online platforms. Power Query provides a unified and user-friendly interface for importing data, regardless of the source. Before we delve into the practical aspects of loading data, let's understand the different sources from which you can load data:

1. Database Sources: This includes relational databases like Microsoft SQL Server, MySQL, and Oracle. You can connect to tables, views, or stored procedures to extract data.

2. File Sources: You can load data from file formats such as Excel workbooks, CSV files, XML, JSON, and more. These files can be stored locally or in cloud storage.

3. Web Data Sources: Data from websites and web services can be loaded into Power Query. This encompasses HTML tables, JSON responses from REST APIs, and other web data formats.

4. Online Services: Online platforms and services, such as Azure Data Lake Storage, SharePoint Online, and social media networks, offer APIs for data access and can be integrated into Power Query.

Loading Data into Power Query:

Now, let's delve into the practical steps involved in loading data into Power Query:

1. Data Source Selection: The first step is to select the data source. This involves identifying the specific source you wish to connect to, such as a database, file, web service, or online platform. For example, you can choose a Microsoft SQL Server database, an Excel file, or a REST API.

2. Connection Details: Depending on the data source, you will need to provide connection details. For databases, this may include the server address, authentication method, and database name. For files, you specify the file path, and for web services, you need to provide the URL or API endpoint.

3. Authentication and Authorization: Some data sources require authentication and authorization. You may need to input credentials, API keys, access tokens, or other security measures to establish a connection securely.

4. Data Retrieval: Once the connection is established, you can retrieve data from the selected source. This typically involves selecting specific tables, views, files, or datasets that you want to import into Power Query.

5. Query Editor: After loading the data, you enter the Query Editor, which is the workspace for data transformation. Here, you can perform operations like filtering, sorting, removing columns, and renaming columns to shape the data as needed.

6. Data Loading Options: Once the data is transformed, you can choose how to load it into your Power BI report or Excel workbook. You can load it directly, create a connection-only query for further transformations, or load it into the data model for analysis.

Illustrative Examples:

Let's provide examples to illustrate the data loading process:

Example 1 - Loading Data from an Excel File:

Suppose you have an Excel workbook named "SalesData.xlsx" with a worksheet named "Sales." To load data from this file into Power Query:

1. Select the file source as an Excel workbook.

2. Provide the file path, e.g., "C:\Path\to\SalesData.xlsx."

3. Choose the "Sales" worksheet.

4. In the Query Editor, you can apply data transformations like filtering rows, removing unwanted columns, and renaming columns.

Example 2 - Loading Data from a Database:

For loading data from a Microsoft SQL Server database, you would follow these steps:

1. Select the database source as SQL Server.

2. Provide the server address, database name, and authentication details.

3. Choose the specific table or view you want to import.

4. In the Query Editor, you can perform data transformations like aggregating sales by date and converting data types.

Conclusion:

Loading data into Power Query is the foundational step in the data transformation process within Power BI and Excel. Understanding the data source, connecting to it, and retrieving data are essential skills for data professionals. This chapter has equipped you with the knowledge and practical skills needed to load data effectively, enabling you to initiate your data transformation journey and harness the power of Power Query for your data-driven projects.

3.2 Basic Data Transformations

In this section, we will explore the essential process of applying basic data transformations within Power Query. Basic data transformations are the core operations that allow you to clean, reshape, and prepare your data for analysis and reporting in Power BI and Excel. This chapter will provide a detailed guide on how to perform basic data transformations using Power Query, along with practical examples to illustrate each concept.

Understanding Basic Data Transformations:

Basic data transformations are the initial set of operations you apply to your data in Power Query. These transformations are essential for cleaning and structuring the data, making it suitable for your analysis or reporting needs. Before we delve into the specific transformation techniques, let's understand the primary types of basic data transformations you may encounter:

1. Filtering Rows: Filtering allows you to include or exclude rows based on specific criteria. You can remove duplicate rows, filter by date ranges, or focus on a subset of data that meets your requirements.

2. Sorting Data: Sorting arranges data in a specific order, which can be useful for visualizing data or organizing it for further analysis. You can sort data by ascending or descending order based on one or multiple columns.

3. Column Operations: You can perform various operations on columns, such as renaming columns to make them more descriptive, adding calculated columns, or removing columns that are not needed for your analysis.

4. Data Type Conversions: Data type conversions allow you to ensure that data is in the correct format for analysis. For example, you can convert text to numbers, dates to the correct date format, or change data types to match your needs.

5. Text Transformations: Text transformations include tasks like converting text to uppercase or lowercase, trimming leading and trailing spaces, and replacing specific characters within text columns.

Basic Data Transformations in Power Query:

Now, let's delve into the practical steps involved in performing basic data transformations in Power Query:

1. Filtering Rows: To filter rows, you can use the filter options in Power Query to include or exclude rows that meet specific criteria. For example, you can filter a sales dataset to only include orders from the current year.

2. Sorting Data: Sorting data is achieved by selecting one or more columns and choosing whether to sort in ascending or descending order. This can help you organize your data for easier analysis or visualization.

3. Column Operations: You can rename columns by simply right-clicking on a column header and selecting "Rename." Adding calculated columns involves creating custom expressions using Power Query's formula language. For example, you can create a calculated column that computes the total revenue for each order.

4. Data Type Conversions: Data type conversions can be performed through the "Change Type" option in Power Query. You can change a text column to a date type, a decimal number to an integer, or vice versa.

5. Text Transformations: Power Query provides various text transformation options. For instance, you can change text to uppercase or lowercase, trim spaces, or replace specific characters within text columns.

Illustrative Examples:

Let's provide examples to illustrate each of these basic data transformations:

Example 1 - Filtering Rows:

Suppose you have a dataset of customer reviews, and you want to filter the reviews that have a rating of 4 or 5 stars:

1. Open the dataset in Power Query.

2. Use the "Filter Rows" option to include only rows where the rating column is equal to 4 or 5.

Example 2 - Sorting Data:

Imagine you have a sales dataset, and you want to sort it by order date in ascending order:

1. Select the "Order Date" column.

2. Choose the "Sort Ascending" option.

Example 3 - Column Operations:

In the same sales dataset, you want to rename the "Revenue" column to "Total Sales":

1. Right-click the "Revenue" column header and select "Rename."

2. Enter the new column name as "Total Sales."

Example 4 - Data Type Conversions:

You have a dataset with dates stored as text, and you want to convert them to the date data type:

1. Select the date column.

2. Use the "Change Type" option and select "Date."

Example 5 - Text Transformations:

Suppose you have a product description column, and you want to convert the text to uppercase:

1. Select the text column.

2. Choose the "Transform" option and select "Uppercase."

Conclusion:

Basic data transformations are the cornerstone of preparing your data for analysis and reporting in Power Query. Whether you're filtering rows, sorting data, performing column operations, converting data types, or transforming text, these operations are fundamental to ensuring that your data is clean, structured, and ready for further processing. This chapter has equipped you with the knowledge and practical skills needed to perform these basic data transformations effectively, enabling you to make the most of Power Query in your data-driven projects.

3.3 Advanced Transformations with the Formula Language (M)

In this section, we will explore the powerful capabilities of advanced data transformations using the Formula Language (M) within Power Query. The Formula Language (M) empowers you to perform complex and tailored data transformations that go beyond basic operations. This chapter will provide a comprehensive guide on how to leverage the Formula Language (M) to address specific data transformation challenges, along with practical examples to illustrate its applications.

Understanding Advanced Transformations with the Formula Language (M):

Advanced data transformations often require a level of specificity that basic transformations may not cover. The Formula Language (M), also known as "M," is a functional language used within Power Query to define custom data transformations. M is particularly useful when you need to perform complex operations, create custom calculations, and manipulate data structures. Before delving into specific applications, it's important to understand the types of advanced transformations that can be achieved with M:

1. Custom Column Formulas: M enables you to create custom formulas for calculated columns. These formulas can include conditional logic, mathematical calculations, and string manipulations.

2. Table Transformations: With M, you can perform table-level transformations, such as merging tables, pivoting and unpivoting data, and aggregating data at different granularities.

3. Combining Queries: M allows you to combine data from multiple queries and data sources, including merging, appending, and joining tables with complex criteria.

4. Error Handling: You can use M to implement error handling logic, such as handling missing values or addressing data quality issues during data transformation.

5. Data Structure Manipulation: M provides tools for reshaping data structures, converting data types, and dealing with hierarchical data like JSON or XML.

Advanced Transformations with the Formula Language (M) in Power Query:

Now, let's delve into the practical steps involved in applying advanced transformations with the Formula Language (M) in Power Query:

1. Custom Column Formulas: To create custom column formulas with M, you can use the "Add Custom Column" option in Power Query. This opens the formula bar, where you can write M expressions to perform advanced calculations. For example, you can create a calculated column that computes a rolling average over a time series dataset.

2. Table Transformations: For table-level transformations, M allows you to use functions like Table.Combine, Table.Pivot, Table.Unpivot, and Table.Group to reshape and aggregate data. For instance, you can pivot a table with data for multiple years into a structure that's suitable for time series analysis.

3. Combining Queries: M provides functions like Table.Join, Table.Merge, and Table.Combine to combine data from multiple queries or data sources. You can join tables based on common keys or merge data from different sources into a consolidated dataset.

4. Error Handling: M includes functions for error handling, such as Table.ReplaceErrors, Table.Clean, and Text.Clean, which help address data quality issues and missing or erroneous values.

5. Data Structure Manipulation: You can use M functions like Json.Document and Xml.Tables to parse and manipulate hierarchical data structures like JSON or XML. This allows you to extract specific elements and transform them into tabular data.

Illustrative Examples:

Let's provide examples to illustrate the application of advanced transformations with the Formula Language (M):

Example 1 - Custom Column Formulas:

Suppose you have a dataset of sales transactions, and you want to calculate the profit margin for each transaction. You can use a custom column formula in M to create a "Profit Margin" column:

1. Use the "Add Custom Column" option in Power Query.

2. Write an M expression that calculates the profit margin as (Profit / Revenue) * 100.

Example 2 - Table Transformations:

Imagine you have a dataset with customer orders, and you want to pivot the data to show the total sales for each product in different years:

1. Use the Table.Pivot function in M to pivot the data by the "Year" column.

2. Define the aggregation function as "Sum" for the sales values.

Example 3 - Combining Queries:

For combining data from multiple sources, consider the scenario where you have sales data in one query and customer information in another query, and you want to combine them based on a common "Customer ID" column:

1. Use the Table.Join function in M to join the sales and customer queries.

2. Specify the matching column as "Customer ID" and the join type (e.g., inner join).

Example 4 - Error Handling:

Suppose you have a dataset with text data that may contain missing values or errors. You can use the Table.Clean function in M to handle these issues:

1. Apply the Table.Clean function to remove any rows with missing or error-prone data.

Example 5 - Data Structure Manipulation:

For hierarchical data, consider a JSON dataset containing product information. You can use the Json.Document function in M to parse the JSON data and extract specific product details:

1. Apply the Json.Document function to parse the JSON data.

2. Use the resulting table to select and transform product attributes.

Conclusion:

Advanced data transformations with the Formula Language (M) in Power Query provide the flexibility and precision needed to address complex data transformation challenges. Whether you're creating custom column formulas, reshaping tables, combining queries, handling errors, or manipulating data structures, M empowers you to tailor your data to your specific needs. This chapter has equipped you with the knowledge and practical skills needed to leverage the Formula Language (M) effectively, enabling you to excel in your data transformation and analysis projects within Power BI and Excel.

3.4 Data Types and Type Conversions

In this section, we will explore the critical aspect of managing data types and performing type conversions within Power Query. Understanding data types and their conversions is essential for ensuring data accuracy, compatibility, and consistency in Power BI and Excel. This chapter will provide an in-depth guide on working with data types and performing type conversions, complemented by practical examples to illustrate their significance.

Understanding Data Types and Type Conversions:

Data types in Power Query define the format and structure of values within your dataset. Managing data types is crucial because it affects how data is treated, sorted, and used in calculations. Data may arrive in different formats, and it's common to encounter scenarios where type conversions are necessary. Before we delve into specific applications, let's grasp the key concepts related to data types and type conversions:

1. Common Data Types: Common data types include Text, Number (Decimal and Integer), Date, Time, Date/Time, Boolean, and Currency. Each data type has specific properties and behaviors.

2. Implicit and Explicit Type Conversions: Implicit type conversions occur automatically when Power Query attempts to convert one data type to another without explicit instruction. Explicit

type conversions are carried out through user-defined operations, ensuring data type precision and accuracy.

3. Handling Data Type Mismatches: Data may arrive with mismatches between expected and actual data types. Handling these mismatches is critical to avoid errors and ensure data consistency.

4. Type Conversion Functions: Power Query provides functions for type conversions. Functions like Text.From, Number.From, Date.From, and List.Transform allow you to change data types explicitly.

Data Types and Type Conversions in Power Query:

Now, let's delve into the practical steps involved in managing data types and performing type conversions within Power Query:

1. Understanding Data Types: Begin by understanding the data types present in your dataset. Power Query automatically detects data types when you load data, but you should verify and, if necessary, adjust them in the Query Editor.

2. Implicit Type Conversions: Be aware of when implicit type conversions occur. For example, when you perform arithmetic operations on columns with different data types, Power Query will attempt implicit conversions to ensure consistent types.

3. Explicit Type Conversions: For explicit type conversions, you can use functions like Text.From, Number.From, Date.From, and others based on the conversion you need to perform. For instance, you can convert a text column containing numbers to a numeric data type using Number.From.

4. Handling Data Type Mismatches: When data types in your dataset don't match your expectations, you can use type conversion functions to rectify the mismatches. For instance, if a date column is stored as text, you can convert it to a date data type using Date.From.

Illustrative Examples:

Let's provide examples to illustrate the significance of data types and type conversions in Power Query:

Example 1 - Managing Date Types:

Suppose you have a dataset with a "Transaction Date" column, and the dates are stored as text. To ensure correct date operations and analysis, you can perform explicit type conversion:

1. In the Query Editor, select the "Transaction Date" column.

2. Use the "Change Type" option and select "Date" to convert the text values to date data type.

Example 2 - Dealing with Numeric Data:

Imagine you have a dataset with a "Price" column containing numbers stored as text. To perform arithmetic operations and calculations, you can explicitly convert the data type:

1. Select the "Price" column in the Query Editor.

2. Use the "Change Type" option and select "Decimal Number" to convert the text values to numeric data type.

Example 3 - Handling Boolean Values:

Suppose your dataset contains a column named "IsAvailable," and the values are stored as "Yes" and "No." To work with Boolean values, you can perform explicit type conversion:

1. Select the "IsAvailable" column in the Query Editor.

2. Use the "Replace Values" option to replace "Yes" with "true" and "No" with "false."

Example 4 - Working with Currency Data:

For a dataset containing currency values in a column labeled "Price," you may need to perform type conversion to ensure compatibility with currency calculations:

1. Select the "Price" column in the Query Editor.

2. Use the "Change Type" option and select "Currency" to convert the numeric values to currency data type.

Conclusion:

Data types and type conversions are pivotal in ensuring data accuracy, consistency, and compatibility in Power Query. Understanding data types, managing implicit and explicit type conversions, and addressing data type mismatches are essential for data preparation and analysis. This chapter has equipped you with the knowledge and practical skills needed to work with data types and perform type conversions effectively, enabling you to handle diverse datasets and maximize the value of your data in Power BI and Excel.

3.5 Data Cleansing and Quality Assurance

In this section, we will explore the crucial processes of data cleansing and quality assurance within Power Query. Data quality is paramount for accurate analysis and reporting in Power BI and Excel. This chapter will provide a comprehensive guide on how to cleanse and ensure the quality of your data, accompanied by practical examples to illustrate best practices.

Understanding Data Cleansing and Quality Assurance:

Data cleansing, also known as data scrubbing or data cleaning, is the process of identifying and correcting errors, inconsistencies, and inaccuracies within your dataset. Quality assurance, on the other hand, involves a series of steps and practices to maintain high data quality throughout your data transformation journey. Before we delve into specific techniques, it's essential to comprehend the significance of data cleansing and quality assurance:

1. Data Cleansing Objectives: The primary objectives of data cleansing include identifying and rectifying data errors, such as missing values, duplicate records, incorrect data types, and outliers. The goal is to ensure that the data is accurate, complete, and consistent.

2. Quality Assurance Practices: Quality assurance encompasses practices like data profiling, data validation, and data monitoring. These practices are aimed at preventing data quality issues from arising and continuously ensuring data integrity.

3. Common Data Quality Issues: Data quality issues can manifest as missing data, inconsistent formatting, outliers, conflicting values, and inaccuracies. Addressing these issues is essential to make informed decisions based on reliable data.

4. Data Cleansing Techniques: Data cleansing techniques include handling missing values, removing duplicates, correcting data types, standardizing formatting, and dealing with outliers. Power Query offers a variety of tools and functions to perform these tasks.

Data Cleansing and Quality Assurance Techniques in Power Query:

Now, let's delve into the practical steps involved in data cleansing and quality assurance within Power Query:

1. Handling Missing Values: Missing values can lead to inaccurate analysis. In Power Query, you can use functions like Table.FillDown, Table.FillUp, or Table.ReplaceValues to manage missing data by filling or replacing them with appropriate values.

2. Removing Duplicates: Duplicate records can skew your analysis. You can use the Remove Duplicates feature in Power Query to eliminate duplicate rows based on specific columns, ensuring data consistency.

3. Data Type Correction: Incorrect data types can lead to errors. You can use functions like Table.TransformColumnTypes to correct data types. For example, convert text data to numeric or date data types as needed.

4. Standardizing Formatting: Inconsistent formatting can affect data integrity. Use text transformation functions like Text.Clean, Text.Trim, and Text.Proper to standardize text values, remove extra spaces, or capitalize text consistently.

5. Handling Outliers: Outliers can distort analysis results. Implement filtering or data transformation operations to manage or exclude outliers from your dataset, ensuring data accuracy.

Illustrative Examples:

Let's provide examples to illustrate the importance of data cleansing and quality assurance techniques in Power Query:

Example 1 - Handling Missing Values:

Suppose you have a dataset of customer information, and some records have missing values in the "Phone Number" column. You can use Power Query to fill missing phone numbers with a default value:

1. Select the "Phone Number" column.

2. Use the Table.FillDown function to fill missing values with a default phone number.

Example 2 - Removing Duplicates:

Imagine you have a sales dataset, and it contains duplicate records for the same sales transactions. To ensure data consistency, you can remove duplicates:

1. Use the "Remove Duplicates" feature in Power Query.

2. Select the relevant columns, such as "Order ID" and "Transaction Date," to identify and remove duplicate records.

Example 3 - Data Type Correction:

For a dataset containing date values stored as text, you may need to correct the data types for accurate date calculations:

1. Select the date column.

2. Use the Table.TransformColumnTypes function to convert the text data to the date data type.

Example 4 - Standardizing Formatting:

Suppose your dataset includes a "Product Name" column with inconsistent capitalization. You can standardize the formatting to ensure uniformity:

1. Select the "Product Name" column.

2. Use the Text.Proper function to capitalize the text consistently.

Example 5 - Handling Outliers:

In a dataset of employee salaries, you may encounter outlier values that need to be addressed to maintain data accuracy:

1. Apply a filter operation to exclude salary values that fall outside a predefined range, ensuring that outliers do not distort salary analysis.

Conclusion:

Data cleansing and quality assurance are essential processes in ensuring data accuracy, consistency, and reliability in Power Query. By addressing missing values, removing duplicates, correcting data types, standardizing formatting, and handling outliers, you can enhance data integrity and make informed decisions based on high-quality data. This chapter has equipped you with the knowledge and practical skills needed to apply data cleansing and quality assurance techniques effectively, enabling you to harness the full potential of Power Query in your data-driven projects within Power BI and Excel.

CHAPTER II
Advanced Power Query Techniques

Part 4. Combining and Appending Queries

4.1 Joining Tables with Relationships

In this section, we will dive into the powerful techniques of joining tables with relationships in Power Query. Creating meaningful relationships between tables is fundamental for data analysis and reporting in Power BI and Excel. This chapter will provide an extensive guide on how to join tables using relationships, complete with practical examples to illustrate the concepts effectively.

Understanding Joining Tables with Relationships:

Joining tables with relationships involves establishing connections between two or more tables based on common columns, also known as keys or foreign keys. These relationships enable you to combine data from multiple sources or tables to create a unified dataset for analysis and reporting. Before we delve into specific techniques, let's grasp the key concepts related to joining tables with relationships:

1. Types of Relationships: There are different types of relationships, including one-to-one, one-to-many, and many-to-many. Each type defines how data is related between tables.

2. Primary and Foreign Keys: In a relationship, one table typically contains the primary key, while the other table contains the foreign key. The primary key is a unique identifier, and the foreign key references the primary key in another table.

3. Data Modeling: Data modeling is the process of defining and managing relationships between tables. It involves identifying the right tables to connect and establishing the appropriate relationships.

4. Benefits of Relationships: Establishing relationships enables you to perform advanced data analysis, create interactive reports, and leverage features like DAX (Data Analysis Expressions) for calculations.

Joining Tables with Relationships in Power Query:

Now, let's delve into the practical steps involved in joining tables with relationships in Power Query:

1. Identifying Common Columns: Begin by identifying the common columns between the tables you want to join. These common columns serve as the basis for establishing relationships.

2. Creating Relationships: In Power Query, you can create relationships by using the "Join" or "Merge" options. The choice of which to use depends on the type of relationship you want to establish.

3. Types of Relationships:

   - One-to-One Relationship: When each record in the primary table is related to a single record in the related table.

   - One-to-Many Relationship: When each record in the primary table is related to multiple records in the related table.

- Many-to-Many Relationship: When records in both tables can have multiple related records in the other table.

4. Managing Relationships: It's essential to manage and maintain relationships, including addressing issues like cardinality, referential integrity, and filtering options.

Illustrative Examples:

Let's provide examples to illustrate the process of joining tables with relationships in Power Query:

Example 1 - One-to-One Relationship:

Suppose you have a "Customers" table and an "Orders" table. Each customer has a unique CustomerID, and each order has a corresponding CustomerID. You can establish a one-to-one relationship based on the common CustomerID column.

1. In Power Query, select the "Customers" table.

2. Use the "Join" or "Merge" option to connect it to the "Orders" table based on the CustomerID column.

Example 2 - One-to-Many Relationship:

Imagine you have a "Departments" table and an "Employees" table. Each department has a unique DepartmentID, and each employee's record includes a DepartmentID indicating their department. You can establish a one-to-many relationship.

1. Select the "Departments" table.

2. Use the "Join" or "Merge" option to connect it to the "Employees" table based on the DepartmentID column.

Example 3 - Many-to-Many Relationship:

For a scenario involving products and categories, where a product can belong to multiple categories, you can create a many-to-many relationship.

1. Create an intermediate table connecting products and categories, indicating which products belong to which categories.

2. Establish relationships between the product table and the intermediate table, as well as between the category table and the intermediate table.

Conclusion:

Joining tables with relationships in Power Query is a fundamental step in creating robust data models for analysis and reporting in Power BI and Excel. Whether you're dealing with one-to-one, one-to-many, or many-to-many relationships, understanding the principles of data modeling and creating relationships between tables enables you to unlock the full potential of your data. This chapter has equipped you with the knowledge and practical skills needed to establish and manage relationships effectively, empowering you to enhance your data analysis capabilities and create insightful reports.

Here's a step-by-step guide on how to join tables with relationships in Power Query:

Step 1: Identifying Common Columns

Before creating relationships, you need to identify the common columns that will serve as the basis for joining tables. In most cases, these columns are unique identifiers, such as CustomerID, OrderID, DepartmentID, or ProductID, that exist in both tables.

Step 2: Launch Power Query

Open Power Query in Power BI or Excel. To do this, go to the "Data" or "Power Query" tab in Excel, or open Power BI Desktop and access the "Edit Queries" option.

Step 3: Select the Primary Table

In Power Query, start by selecting the primary table. This is the table you want to create a relationship from. In our examples, this could be the "Customers" table or the "Departments" table.

Step 4: Choose the Join or Merge Option

You have two main options for joining tables: "Join" and "Merge."

- Join: Use this option for one-to-one or one-to-many relationships. It's suitable when each record in the primary table corresponds to one or multiple records in the related table. To use this option:

   - Select the primary table.

   - Find the "Join" option (it may be labeled as "Join Queries" or "Join Tables").

   - Specify the related table and the common column (e.g., CustomerID or DepartmentID) as the matching key.

   - Define the type of join you want to create (e.g., inner, left outer, right outer, full outer).

- Merge: Use this option for many-to-many relationships or more complex scenarios. It's suitable when records in both tables can have multiple related records in the other table. To use this option:

  - Select the primary table.

  - Find the "Merge Queries" or "Append Queries" option.

  - Specify the related table and the common column (e.g., ProductID) as the matching key.

  - Define the type of merge you want to create (e.g., inner, left outer, right outer, full outer).

Step 5: Manage the Relationship

After creating the relationship, it's crucial to manage and maintain it. You may need to address issues related to cardinality, referential integrity, and filtering options. These settings can be configured in Power Query to ensure the relationship works as expected.

Step 6: Load Data

Once you've established and configured the relationships, you can load the data into your Power BI or Excel workbook. The related tables will now be connected, and you can use them for data analysis, report creation, and leveraging DAX calculations as needed.

Remember to save your Power Query changes, and the relationships will persist in your Power BI or Excel project.

This step-by-step guide should help you understand how to join tables with relationships in Power Query for effective data modeling and analysis.

4.2 Merging Queries

In this section, we'll explore the advanced technique of merging queries in Power Query, which is a powerful feature for combining and consolidating data from multiple tables or queries into a single, unified dataset. Merging queries is an essential skill for data transformation and preparation in Power BI and Excel, and this chapter will provide a detailed guide on how to perform query merging, complete with practical examples to illustrate the concepts effectively.

Understanding Merging Queries:

Merging queries involves the process of combining data from two or more tables or queries based on a common column or set of columns. This allows you to consolidate related information from different data sources and tables into a single dataset, making it easier for analysis and reporting. Before we dive into the practical aspects, let's grasp the key concepts related to merging queries:

1. Primary and Related Tables: When merging queries, you typically have a primary table and one or more related tables. The primary table is the target where you want to combine data, and the related tables provide the additional information you want to append.

2. Common Columns: Merging queries relies on common columns between the primary and related tables. These common columns serve as matching keys to determine how data should be combined.

3. Types of Merges: There are different types of merges you can perform:

  - Inner Join: Combines only the matching rows from both tables, discarding non-matching rows.

  - Left Outer Join: Combines all rows from the primary table and matching rows from the related table. Non-matching rows from the primary table are included with null values from the related table.

- Right Outer Join: Similar to the left outer join, but it includes all rows from the related table and matching rows from the primary table.

- Full Outer Join: Combines all rows from both tables, including matching and non-matching rows.

Merging Queries in Power Query:

Now, let's dive into the practical steps involved in merging queries using Power Query:

1. Open Power Query: Launch Power Query in Power BI or Excel by going to the "Data" or "Power Query" tab and selecting "Edit Queries."

2. Select the Primary Table: Begin by selecting the primary table where you want to combine data. This is the table that will receive the additional information from the related table(s).

3. Choose the Merge Option: In Power Query, locate the "Merge Queries" or "Join Queries" option, depending on your version. This option allows you to specify the related table and the common column(s) you want to use for the merge.

4. Configure the Merge: When configuring the merge, you'll define the type of join you want to perform (inner, left outer, right outer, or full outer). You'll also specify the related table and the common column(s) for matching.

5. Review and Transform Data: After the merge, Power Query will present you with a preview of the combined data. You can further transform, filter, or manipulate the data as needed.

Illustrative Examples:

Let's provide examples to illustrate the process of merging queries in Power Query:

Example 1 - Inner Join:

Suppose you have a "Customers" table and an "Orders" table. You want to combine customer information with order details where there's a matching CustomerID.

1. Select the "Customers" table.

2. Use the "Merge Queries" option to connect it to the "Orders" table based on the CustomerID column.

3. Choose an inner join to include only matching customer and order records.

Example 2 - Left Outer Join:

Imagine you have a "Departments" table and an "Employees" table. You want to include all department records and related employee information, where the DepartmentID matches.

1. Select the "Departments" table.

2. Use the "Merge Queries" option to connect it to the "Employees" table based on the DepartmentID column.

3. Choose a left outer join to include all departments and match them with employee records where applicable.

Example 3 - Full Outer Join:

For a scenario involving product categories and product details, you want to include all categories and their associated products.

1. Select the "Categories" table.

2. Use the "Merge Queries" option to connect it to the "Products" table based on the CategoryID column.

3. Choose a full outer join to include all categories and products, matching where relevant.

Conclusion:

Merging queries in Power Query is a valuable technique for consolidating and combining data from multiple sources or tables, enabling you to create a unified dataset for analysis and reporting in Power BI and Excel. Whether you're performing inner joins, left outer joins, right outer joins, or full outer joins, understanding the principles of merging queries empowers you to efficiently transform and shape your data for insightful data analysis and reporting. This chapter has provided a comprehensive guide and practical examples to help you master the art of merging queries and harness the full potential of your data.

Here's a step-by-step guide on how to merge queries in Power Query:

Step 1: Open Power Query

- Launch Power Query in either Power BI or Excel. You can do this by going to the "Data" or "Power Query" tab and selecting "Edit Queries."

Step 2: Select the Primary Table

- Start by selecting the primary table where you want to combine the data. This is the table that will receive the additional information from the related table(s).

Step 3: Choose the Merge Option

- Locate the "Merge Queries" or "Join Queries" option within Power Query. The exact label may vary depending on your version of Power Query.

Step 4: Configure the Merge

- When configuring the merge, follow these steps:

  - Specify the related table that you want to merge with the primary table.

  - Select the common column(s) that you want to use for matching between the two tables.

  - Choose the type of merge you want to perform:

    - Inner Join: Combines only the matching rows from both tables, discarding non-matching rows.

    - Left Outer Join: Combines all rows from the primary table and matching rows from the related table. Non-matching rows from the primary table are included with null values from the related table.

    - Right Outer Join: Similar to the left outer join, but it includes all rows from the related table and matching rows from the primary table.

    - Full Outer Join: Combines all rows from both tables, including matching and non-matching rows.

Step 5: Review and Transform Data

- After the merge, Power Query will display a preview of the combined data. You can review and further transform, filter, or manipulate the data as needed.

Step 6: Load Data

- Once you've successfully merged the queries and made any necessary transformations, you can load the combined data into your Power BI or Excel workbook. This data is now ready for analysis and reporting.

Step 7: Save Changes

- Don't forget to save your Power Query changes to ensure that the merged queries and relationships persist in your Power BI or Excel project.

By following these steps, you'll be able to effectively merge queries in Power Query, combining and consolidating data from multiple tables or queries into a single, unified dataset for your data analysis and reporting needs.

4.3 Appending Queries

In this section, we'll delve into the technique of appending queries in Power Query, a powerful feature that allows you to stack or concatenate data from multiple tables or queries vertically. Appending queries is a fundamental aspect of data transformation and preparation in Power BI and Excel. This chapter provides a comprehensive guide on how to append queries, complete with practical examples to clarify the concept effectively.

Understanding Appending Queries:

Appending queries involves the process of stacking or combining data from different tables or queries, typically with identical structures, vertically. The result is a single, consolidated dataset where rows from multiple tables are appended one below the other. This is especially useful when dealing with datasets that are split into multiple files or tables. Before we get into the practical aspects, let's understand the key concepts related to appending queries:

1. Primary and Related Queries: When appending queries, you have a primary query (or table) and one or more related queries that you want to append. The primary query is the target where the data will be appended.

2. Identical Structure: The queries or tables you intend to append should have the same structure, including the same columns in the same order.

Appending Queries in Power Query:

Now, let's explore the step-by-step process of appending queries using Power Query:

Step 1: Open Power Query

- Launch Power Query in Power BI or Excel by accessing the "Data" or "Power Query" tab and selecting "Edit Queries."

Step 2: Select the Primary Query

- Start by selecting the primary query, which is the one where you want to append data. This is the target for the appended data.

Step 3: Choose the Append Option

- In Power Query, find the "Append Queries" or "Combine Queries" option, depending on your version. This option allows you to specify the related queries that you want to append.

Step 4: Configure the Append

- When configuring the append operation, follow these steps:

  - Specify the related queries that you want to append to the primary query.

  - Ensure that the related queries have the same column structure as the primary query.

  - Review the preview of the appended data to ensure it aligns with your expectations.

Step 5: Review and Transform Data

- After the append operation, you'll see a preview of the combined data. You can review and further transform, filter, or manipulate the appended data as needed.

Step 6: Load Data

- Once you've successfully appended the queries and made any necessary transformations, you can load the combined data into your Power BI or Excel workbook. This data is now ready for analysis and reporting.

Step 7: Save Changes

- Make sure to save your Power Query changes to ensure the appended queries are part of your Power BI or Excel project.

Illustrative Examples:

Let's provide examples to illustrate the process of appending queries in Power Query:

Example 1 - Appending Similar Monthly Sales Data:

Suppose you have separate tables for monthly sales data, each with the same column structure (Date, Product, Sales). You want to stack these tables to create a single, unified sales dataset.

1. Select one of the monthly sales tables as the primary query.

2. Use the "Append Queries" option to connect and append the remaining monthly sales tables.

Example 2 - Appending Multiple Excel Files:

Imagine you have multiple Excel files, each containing the same type of data (e.g., customer information). You want to combine the data from these files into one dataset.

1. Select the data from one of the Excel files as the primary query.

2. Use the "Append Queries" option to append data from the other Excel files.

Conclusion:

Appending queries in Power Query is a vital technique for consolidating data from multiple tables or queries with identical structures, allowing you to create a unified dataset for efficient data analysis and reporting in Power BI and Excel. Whether you're dealing with monthly sales data, multiple Excel files, or any similar data sources, understanding the principles of appending queries empowers you to transform and shape your data effectively. This chapter provides a comprehensive guide and practical examples to help you master the art of appending queries and utilize it for enhancing your data analysis capabilities and creating insightful reports.

4.4 Appending Queries

In this section, we'll explore the advanced technique of combining data from multiple sources in Power Query. This feature empowers you to gather and integrate data from various origins, such as databases, web services, and local files, into a cohesive dataset for analysis in Power BI and Excel. This chapter provides a comprehensive guide on how to combine data from multiple sources, complete with practical examples to clarify the concept effectively.

Understanding Combining Data from Multiple Sources:

Combining data from multiple sources entails the process of aggregating information from diverse origins into a single, unified dataset for streamlined data analysis and reporting. This technique is indispensable when dealing with complex analyses that require data from disparate data stores. Before we delve into the practical aspects, let's grasp the key concepts related to combining data from multiple sources:

1. Data Sources: When combining data from multiple sources, you may need to connect to various types of data stores, including databases, web services, local files (e.g., Excel, CSV), and more.

2. Data Retrieval: You'll extract data from these sources using Power Query's extensive connectivity options.

3. Data Transformation: After retrieving data, you can perform necessary transformations, cleansing, and data shaping to align data from different sources.

Combining Data from Multiple Sources in Power Query:

Now, let's explore the step-by-step process of combining data from multiple sources using Power Query:

Step 1: Open Power Query

- Launch Power Query in Power BI or Excel by accessing the "Data" or "Power Query" tab and selecting "Edit Queries."

Step 2: Connect to Data Sources

- Utilize Power Query's broad array of connectors to establish connections to the various data sources you wish to combine. These may include databases, web services, and local files. Configure each connection as required, providing credentials and query specifics.

Step 3: Retrieve and Transform Data

- Retrieve data from each source and perform necessary transformations using Power Query's intuitive tools. This step may involve filtering, sorting, renaming columns, or dealing with data types to ensure consistency across sources.

Step 4: Append or Merge Queries

- Depending on the nature of your data and the relationships between sources, you can use either the "Append Queries" or "Merge Queries" feature to combine the data. The choice between appending and merging depends on the structure and relationships of the data sources. If the sources have a similar structure, appending may be appropriate; if there are relationships to establish, merging may be more suitable.

Step 5: Review and Transform Combined Data

- After appending or merging the queries, review the combined data in Power Query. You may need to perform additional transformations or adjustments to ensure data consistency and accuracy.

Step 6: Load Data

- Once you are satisfied with the combined dataset, load it into your Power BI or Excel workbook. The integrated data is now ready for in-depth analysis and reporting.

Step 7: Save Changes

- Don't forget to save your Power Query changes to ensure that the combined data from multiple sources is part of your Power BI or Excel project.

Illustrative Examples:

Let's provide examples to illustrate the process of combining data from multiple sources in Power Query:

Example 1 - Combining Data from an External Database and a Web Service:

Imagine you need to combine customer information from an external SQL database with real-time sales data from a web service. You would first connect to the SQL database, retrieve customer data, connect to the web service, and then combine both datasets for comprehensive analysis.

Example 2 - Combining Data from Local Excel Files:

Suppose you have multiple Excel files containing sales data from different regions. To analyze the consolidated sales data, you'd connect to each Excel file, retrieve the relevant data, and then append the data from all files into a single dataset for an overarching view of sales performance.

Conclusion:

Combining data from multiple sources in Power Query is an essential technique for creating a unified dataset from diverse origins. Whether you're integrating data from external databases, web services, local files, or other sources, mastering the art of combining data empowers you to perform comprehensive data analysis and generate insightful reports in Power BI and Excel. This chapter has provided a comprehensive guide and practical examples to help you harness the capabilities of Power Query for seamless data integration and enhanced data analysis.

Part 5. Conditional Logic and Custom Functions

5.1 Creating Conditional Columns

In this section, we will explore the powerful technique of creating conditional columns in Power Query. Conditional columns enable you to dynamically generate new columns in your dataset based on specified criteria, allowing for data transformation and enrichment. This chapter provides a comprehensive guide on how to create conditional columns, complete with practical examples to illustrate the concept effectively.

Understanding Conditional Columns:

Conditional columns in Power Query provide a way to add new columns to your dataset based on certain conditions or criteria. These conditions can range from simple comparisons to complex logical operations. The resulting column values depend on whether the specified conditions are met. Before we dive into practical examples, let's understand the key concepts related to creating conditional columns:

1. Conditions: Conditions are logical statements or expressions that evaluate to either true or false. You can use a variety of operators (e.g., equals, greater than, less than) and functions to define conditions.

2. Result Values: When a condition is met (true), the corresponding column value is assigned. If the condition is not met (false), another value or operation can be applied.

Creating Conditional Columns in Power Query:

Now, let's explore the step-by-step process of creating conditional columns using Power Query:

Step 1: Open Power Query

- Launch Power Query in Power BI or Excel by accessing the "Data" or "Power Query" tab and selecting "Edit Queries."

Step 2: Select the Source Query

- Start by selecting the source query or table to which you want to add conditional columns.

Step 3: Create Conditional Columns

- Utilize the "Add Conditional Column" option in Power Query to define the conditions and corresponding column values. Follow these steps:

  - Specify a name for the new column.

  - Define the condition using operators, functions, and column references.

  - Assign the value or operation to be applied when the condition is true.

Step 4: Review and Transform Data

- After creating conditional columns, you'll see a preview of the data with the newly added columns. You can review and further transform or manipulate the data as needed.

Step 5: Load Data

- Once you've successfully created conditional columns and made any necessary transformations, load the enhanced dataset into your Power BI or Excel workbook. The data is now ready for analysis and reporting.

Step 6: Save Changes

- Ensure that you save your Power Query changes to preserve the conditional columns as part of your Power BI or Excel project.

Illustrative Examples:

Let's provide examples to illustrate the process of creating conditional columns in Power Query:

Example 1 - Categorizing Sales Data:

Suppose you have a sales dataset with a "Sales Amount" column, and you want to categorize each sale as "Low," "Medium," or "High" based on the sales amount.

1. In Power Query, select the source query containing the sales data.

2. Create a conditional column named "Sales Category" with the following condition:

   - If "Sales Amount" is less than 1000, set the value to "Low."

   - If "Sales Amount" is between 1000 and 5000, set the value to "Medium."

   - If "Sales Amount" is greater than 5000, set the value to "High."

Example 2 - Classifying Customers by Purchase Frequency:

Imagine you have customer data with a "Purchase Count" column, and you want to classify customers as "Infrequent," "Regular," or "Frequent" based on their purchase frequency.

1. In Power Query, select the source query containing the customer data.

2. Create a conditional column named "Customer Category" with the following condition:

   - If "Purchase Count" is less than 5, set the value to "Infrequent."

   - If "Purchase Count" is between 5 and 20, set the value to "Regular."

   - If "Purchase Count" is greater than 20, set the value to "Frequent."

Conclusion:

Creating conditional columns in Power Query is a versatile and invaluable technique for data transformation and enrichment. Whether you're categorizing data, applying labels, or making data-driven decisions, conditional columns empower you to dynamically add context and meaning to your dataset. This chapter has provided a comprehensive guide and practical examples to help you master the art of creating conditional columns and leverage them for enhanced data analysis and reporting capabilities in Power BI and Excel.

Creating Conditional Columns in Power Query - Step-by-Step Guide:

Step 1: Open Power Query

Begin by launching Power Query in Power BI or Excel. You can do this by navigating to the "Data" or "Power Query" tab in your application's menu bar and selecting "Edit Queries."

Step 2: Select the Source Query

In the Power Query Editor, select the source query or table to which you want to add conditional columns. This is the dataset you'll be working with.

Step 3: Create Conditional Columns

1. Click on the "Add Column" tab in the Power Query Editor.

2. From the dropdown menu, select "Conditional Column." This will open a dialog box where you can define the conditions and corresponding column values.

3. In the "New column name" field, specify a name for the new column you're creating.

4. In the "If" section, define the condition that determines when the new column value should be assigned. You can use operators, functions, and references to other columns to create your condition. For example, you can use expressions like [Sales Amount] < 1000 to check if the "Sales Amount" is less than 1000.

5. In the "Then" section, specify the value or operation to be applied to the new column when the condition is true. For instance, you can enter "Low" to categorize sales as "Low" when the condition is met.

6. You can also add additional conditions by clicking the "Add Rule" button and specifying conditions and values for each rule.

Step 4: Review and Transform Data

Once you've defined your conditional columns, the Power Query Editor will show you a preview of the data with the newly added columns. You can review the results and, if needed, perform further data transformations, such as renaming columns or changing data types.

Step 5: Load Data

After you're satisfied with the conditional columns and any other data transformations, click the "Close & Apply" button in the Power Query Editor. This will load the enhanced dataset into your Power BI or Excel workbook, making it ready for analysis and reporting.

Step 6: Save Changes

To preserve your Power Query changes, make sure to save your Power BI or Excel project. This ensures that the conditional columns are integrated into your workbook.

Illustrative Examples:

Here are examples to illustrate how to create conditional columns in Power Query:

Example 1 - Categorizing Sales Data:

1. In Power Query, select the source query with sales data.

2. Create a conditional column named "Sales Category" with the condition: "If [Sales Amount] < 1000, then 'Low'; If [Sales Amount] is between 1000 and 5000, then 'Medium'; If [Sales Amount] > 5000, then 'High'."

Example 2 - Classifying Customers by Purchase Frequency:

1. In Power Query, select the source query with customer data.

2. Create a conditional column named "Customer Category" with the condition: "If [Purchase Count] < 5, then 'Infrequent'; If [Purchase Count] is between 5 and 20, then 'Regular'; If [Purchase Count] > 20, then 'Frequent'."

Conclusion:

Creating conditional columns in Power Query is a versatile and valuable technique for data transformation. It allows you to add context and meaning to your dataset based on specific conditions. Whether you're categorizing data or making data-driven decisions, mastering this technique enhances your data analysis and reporting capabilities in Power BI and Excel.

5.2 Using Custom Functions in Power Query

In this section, we will delve into the powerful world of custom functions in Power Query. Custom functions allow you to extend the capabilities of Power Query by creating your own specialized functions to manipulate and transform data. This chapter provides a comprehensive guide on how to use custom functions in Power Query, complete with practical examples to illustrate the concept effectively.

Understanding Custom Functions:

Custom functions in Power Query are user-defined functions that you create to perform specific tasks on your data. These functions can range from simple operations to complex data transformations, and they can be used to automate repetitive tasks or address unique data requirements. Before we explore practical examples, let's understand the key concepts related to using custom functions:

1. Function Creation: Creating custom functions involves defining the function's behavior, input parameters, and output values. You can use the Power Query Formula Language (M) to write custom function code.

2. Parameterization: Custom functions often accept input parameters that provide flexibility in applying the function to different data scenarios. Parameters can be values, columns, or tables.

3. Function Invocation: Once created, custom functions can be invoked within your queries to transform data. You can use them in combination with existing Power Query functions and steps.

Using Custom Functions in Power Query:

Now, let's explore the step-by-step process of using custom functions in Power Query:

Step 1: Create a Custom Function

- To create a custom function, open Power Query in Power BI or Excel and navigate to the "View" tab. From the "Advanced Editor," you can write custom function code using the Power Query Formula Language (M).

Step 2: Define Function Parameters

- Specify the input parameters required by your custom function. These parameters can be values, columns, or tables, and they allow you to apply the function to different data scenarios.

Step 3: Implement Function Logic

- Write the logic of your custom function, including any data transformations, calculations, or operations it needs to perform. Ensure the function returns the desired output.

Step 4: Invoke the Custom Function

- In your Power Query queries, invoke the custom function using the "Invoke Custom Function" option. Provide the necessary parameters and specify where the function should be applied.

Step 5: Review and Transform Data

- After invoking the custom function, you can see the results in the Power Query Editor. You can further transform the data as needed.

Step 6: Load Data

- Once you're satisfied with the data transformations, load the enhanced dataset into your Power BI or Excel workbook for analysis and reporting.

Step 7: Save Changes

- Ensure that you save your Power Query changes to preserve the custom function as part of your Power BI or Excel project.

Illustrative Examples:

Let's provide examples to illustrate how to use custom functions in Power Query:

Example 1 - Custom Function for Currency Conversion:

Imagine you have a dataset with sales amounts in different currencies, and you want to create a custom function to convert all amounts to a common currency.

1. Create a custom function named "ConvertCurrency" that accepts parameters such as the "Amount," "FromCurrency," and "ToCurrency."

2. Write the function logic to perform the currency conversion, using exchange rates or external data sources.

3. Invoke the "ConvertCurrency" function for each row of data to convert the sales amounts.

Example 2 - Custom Function for Data Validation:

Suppose you have a dataset with dates, and you want to create a custom function to validate if the dates fall within a specified range.

1. Create a custom function named "DateValidation" that accepts parameters like "Date" and "StartDate" and "EndDate."

2. Write the function logic to check if the "Date" is within the specified range.

3. Invoke the "DateValidation" function to validate dates in your dataset.

Conclusion:

Using custom functions in Power Query empowers you to extend its capabilities and perform specialized data transformations. Whether you're creating functions for currency conversion, data validation, or other unique tasks, custom functions allow you to automate and streamline your data preparation process. This chapter has provided a comprehensive guide and practical examples to help you harness the potential of custom functions and enhance your data manipulation and transformation capabilities in Power BI and Excel.

Using Custom Functions in Power Query - Step-by-Step Guide:

Step 1: Create a Custom Function

1. Open Power Query in Power BI or Excel.

2. Go to the "View" tab and click on "Advanced Editor" to access the code editor.

Step 2: Define Function Parameters

1. Inside the code editor, start by defining the input parameters for your custom function. Parameters can be values, columns, or tables, and they provide flexibility in applying the function to different data scenarios.

Step 3: Implement Function Logic

1. Write the logic of your custom function using the Power Query Formula Language (M). This logic should include the data transformations, calculations, or operations you want the function to perform. Ensure that the function returns the desired output.

Step 4: Invoke the Custom Function

1. In your Power Query queries, you can invoke the custom function you created. Use the "Invoke Custom Function" option to do this.

2. Specify the function name, and provide the necessary parameters the function expects. Indicate where the function should be applied in your queries.

Step 5: Review and Transform Data

1. After invoking the custom function, review the results in the Power Query Editor. You can further transform the data as needed, such as renaming columns, changing data types, or applying additional steps.

Step 6: Load Data

1. Once you're satisfied with the data transformations, click the "Close & Apply" button in the Power Query Editor. This loads the enhanced dataset into your Power BI or Excel workbook, making it ready for analysis and reporting.

Step 7: Save Changes

1. To ensure that your Power Query changes, including the custom function, are preserved, save your Power BI or Excel project. This integrates the custom function into your workbook.

Illustrative Examples:

Here are examples to illustrate how to use custom functions in Power Query:

Example 1 - Custom Function for Currency Conversion:

1. Create a custom function named "ConvertCurrency" that accepts parameters like "Amount," "FromCurrency," and "ToCurrency."

2. Write the function logic to perform currency conversion using exchange rates or external data sources.

3. Invoke the "ConvertCurrency" function for each row of data to convert sales amounts.

Example 2 - Custom Function for Data Validation:

1. Create a custom function named "DateValidation" that accepts parameters like "Date," "StartDate," and "EndDate."

2. Write the function logic to check if the "Date" falls within the specified date range.

3. Invoke the "DateValidation" function to validate dates in your dataset.

Conclusion:

Using custom functions in Power Query allows you to extend its capabilities and perform specialized data transformations. Whether you're creating functions for currency conversion, data validation, or other unique tasks, custom functions enable you to automate and streamline your data preparation process. This chapter has provided a comprehensive guide and practical examples to help you leverage the potential of custom functions and enhance your data manipulation and transformation capabilities in Power BI and Excel.

5.3 Error Handling and Validation

In this section, we will explore the essential topic of error handling and data validation within Power Query. Error handling is crucial when working with data, as it helps ensure the quality and reliability of your data transformation processes. This chapter provides a detailed guide on how to implement error handling and validation techniques in Power Query, complete with practical examples for a better understanding.

Understanding Error Handling and Validation:

Error handling and validation are techniques used to identify, handle, and prevent errors in your data during the transformation process. They help ensure that the data is consistent, accurate, and compliant with your requirements. Here are the key concepts related to error handling and validation in Power Query:

1. Error Identification: Power Query can detect errors in data, such as missing values, incorrect data types, or invalid values. Identifying these errors is the first step in the process.

2. Error Handling: Once errors are identified, you can implement error-handling techniques to address them. This may involve replacing missing values, converting data types, or applying specific rules to correct errors.

3. Data Validation: Data validation ensures that your data meets certain criteria or rules. For example, you can validate that dates fall within a specified range or that numeric values are within acceptable limits.

4. Custom Validation Functions: Power Query allows you to create custom validation functions to enforce specific data rules. These functions can be used to check the validity of data based on your requirements.

Implementing Error Handling and Validation in Power Query:

Here is a step-by-step process to implement error handling and validation in Power Query:

Step 1: Identify Errors

1. In Power Query, open the query you want to validate or handle errors for.

2. Use built-in functions such as "Table.SelectColumns" and "Table.AddColumn" to identify errors in your data. For example, you can filter out rows with missing values or incorrect data types.

Step 2: Apply Error Handling

1. To handle errors, use functions like "Table.FillDown" to replace missing values with appropriate data or "Table.TransformColumnTypes" to convert data types as needed.

Step 3: Implement Data Validation

1. Create custom validation functions using the Power Query Formula Language (M) to enforce specific data validation rules. These functions can be simple or complex, depending on your requirements.

Step 4: Invoke Custom Validation Functions

1. Invoke the custom validation functions for your data, either during the initial data load or as part of your data transformation steps.

Step 5: Review and Transform Data

1. After implementing error handling and validation, review the results in the Power Query Editor. Ensure that your data is consistent and complies with your rules.

Step 6: Load Data

1. Once you're satisfied with the error handling and validation processes, load the enhanced dataset into your Power BI or Excel workbook for analysis and reporting.

Step 7: Save Changes

1. Save your Power Query changes to preserve the error handling and validation rules as part of your Power BI or Excel project.

Illustrative Examples:

Here are examples to illustrate error handling and validation in Power Query:

Example 1 - Error Handling for Missing Values:

1. Identify missing values in a "Price" column and use the "Table.FillDown" function to replace missing prices with the last valid value in the column.

Example 2 - Data Validation for Dates:

1. Create a custom validation function named "ValidateDateRange" that checks if dates in a "TransactionDate" column fall within a specified date range.

2. Invoke the "ValidateDateRange" function to validate the date values in your dataset.

Conclusion:

Implementing error handling and data validation in Power Query is essential for maintaining data quality and integrity. These techniques help you identify and address data issues, ensuring that your data is reliable for analysis and reporting. By following the steps outlined in this chapter and utilizing practical examples, you can enhance your data transformation processes and make your data preparation more robust and accurate in Power BI and Excel.

Implementing Error Handling and Data Validation in Power Query - Step-by-Step Guide:

Step 1: Identify Errors

1. Open the query you want to validate or handle errors for in Power Query.

2. Use built-in Power Query functions like "Table.SelectColumns" and "Table.AddColumn" to identify errors in your data. For instance, you can filter out rows with missing values or incorrect data types.

Step 2: Apply Error Handling

1. To handle errors, utilize functions such as "Table.FillDown" to replace missing values with appropriate data or "Table.TransformColumnTypes" to convert data types as required.

Step 3: Implement Data Validation

1. Create custom validation functions using the Power Query Formula Language (M) to enforce specific data validation rules. These functions can range from simple checks like validating date ranges to more complex validations based on your specific requirements.

Step 4: Invoke Custom Validation Functions

1. Invoke the custom validation functions for your data, either during the initial data load or as part of your data transformation steps. Ensure that the functions are applied to the relevant columns.

Step 5: Review and Transform Data

1. After implementing error handling and validation, review the results in the Power Query Editor. Check that your data is consistent and complies with your validation rules.

2. You can further transform your data as needed, such as renaming columns, changing data types, or applying additional steps.

Step 6: Load Data

1. Once you are satisfied with the error handling and validation processes, load the enhanced dataset into your Power BI or Excel workbook. This data will now be suitable for analysis and reporting.

Step 7: Save Changes

1. Don't forget to save your Power Query changes to preserve the error handling and validation rules as part of your Power BI or Excel project.

Illustrative Examples:

Here are examples to illustrate error handling and data validation in Power Query:

Example 1 - Error Handling for Missing Values:

1. Identify missing values in a "Price" column.

2. Use the "Table.FillDown" function to replace missing prices with the last valid value in the column.

Example 2 - Data Validation for Dates:

1. Create a custom validation function named "ValidateDateRange."

2. This function checks if dates in a "TransactionDate" column fall within a specified date range.

3. Invoke the "ValidateDateRange" function to validate the date values in your dataset.

Conclusion:

Implementing error handling and data validation in Power Query is crucial for maintaining data quality and integrity. These techniques help you identify and address data issues, ensuring that your data is reliable for analysis and reporting. By following the steps outlined in this chapter and utilizing practical examples, you can enhance your data transformation processes and make your data preparation more robust and accurate in Power BI and Excel.

Part 6. Grouping, Aggregating, and Pivoting Data

6.1 Grouping Data

In this section, we will delve into the powerful techniques of grouping data in Power Query. Grouping data allows you to organize and analyze information more effectively by creating summary views of your dataset. Whether you want to perform calculations on specific groups, understand data distribution, or create structured reports, mastering the art of data grouping is essential. This chapter provides a comprehensive guide on how to group data effectively, complete with practical examples for a better understanding.

Understanding Data Grouping:

Data grouping is the process of categorizing and organizing data into subsets or groups based on common characteristics or attributes. When you group data, you create a structured hierarchy that allows you to perform aggregate functions and analysis within each group. Here are the key concepts related to data grouping in Power Query:

1. Grouping Criteria: You define the criteria by which data is grouped. For example, you can group sales data by product category, time period, or geographical location.

2. Grouping Results: After grouping, you obtain summary views or tables for each group. These can include subtotals, counts, averages, or any other calculations you need.

3. Aggregate Functions: You can apply aggregate functions like sum, count, average, max, or min to the grouped data. These functions help derive valuable insights within each group.

4. Nested Grouping: You can also perform nested grouping, where data is grouped by multiple criteria. For example, you can group sales data by both product category and time period.

Implementing Data Grouping in Power Query:

Here is a step-by-step process to implement data grouping in Power Query:

Step 1: Select Data for Grouping

1. Open the query containing the data you want to group.

2. Use the "Group By" feature in Power Query to select the columns by which you want to group your data.

Step 2: Define Grouping Criteria

1. Specify the grouping criteria by selecting the columns that will define the groups. You can choose one or more columns, and you can also use custom functions to create grouping criteria.

Step 3: Apply Aggregate Functions

1. For each group, you can apply aggregate functions such as sum, count, average, max, or min to calculate relevant statistics.

2. You can create custom aggregate functions if needed for more complex calculations.

Step 4: Review and Transform Data

1. Review the grouped data and the resulting summary views in the Power Query Editor.

2. Further transform your grouped data, rename columns, or apply additional steps as necessary.

Step 5: Load Data

1. Once you're satisfied with the grouped and aggregated dataset, load it into your Power BI or Excel workbook.

Step 6: Save Changes

1. Save your Power Query changes to preserve the grouping and aggregation rules as part of your project.

Illustrative Examples:

Here are examples to illustrate data grouping in Power Query:

Example 1 - Grouping Sales Data by Product Category:

1. Group sales data by the "Product Category" column.

2. Apply aggregate functions like sum to calculate total sales within each category.

Example 2 - Nested Grouping by Region and Month:

1. Group data by "Region" and then by "Month."

2. Calculate aggregate functions such as sum and count for each region-month combination.

Conclusion:

Data grouping in Power Query is a fundamental skill for data analysis and reporting. By grouping data based on criteria, you can gain deeper insights, perform calculations within specific groups, and create structured reports. This chapter has provided a comprehensive guide and practical examples to help you master the art of data grouping and take your data manipulation and transformation skills to the next level in Power BI and Excel.

Implementing Data Grouping in Power Query - Step-by-Step Guide:

Step 1: Select Data for Grouping

1. Open the Power Query editor in Power BI or Excel, and load the dataset you want to work with.

2. In the Power Query editor, select the query that contains the data you want to group.

3. Locate the "Group By" option in the Power Query editor, typically found in the "Home" or "Transform" tab.

4. Click on "Group By" to initiate the grouping process.

Step 2: Define Grouping Criteria

1. In the "Group By" dialog, you'll see a list of columns from your dataset. Select the columns by which you want to group your data. These columns will be the grouping criteria.

2. You can choose one or more columns as grouping criteria. For example, if you're working with sales data, you can group by "Product Category" and "Region" simultaneously for more detailed insights.

3. You can also create custom grouping criteria by using the "Group By" dialog's formula bar. This allows for more complex grouping based on your specific needs.

Step 3: Apply Aggregate Functions

1. For each group you've defined, you can apply aggregate functions to calculate statistics or perform operations within each group. Common aggregate functions include sum, count, average, max, and min.

2. Select the aggregate functions you need for each grouping criterion, and specify the columns to which these functions should be applied.

3. If your analysis requires custom aggregate functions, you can create and use them within the "Group By" dialog.

Step 4: Review and Transform Data

1. After applying the grouping and aggregate functions, review the grouped data and the resulting summary views in the Power Query editor. This allows you to ensure that the grouping and calculations meet your requirements.

2. You can further transform your grouped data as needed. This might involve renaming columns, changing data types, or applying additional transformation steps.

Step 5: Load Data

1. Once you're satisfied with the grouped and aggregated dataset, load it into your Power BI or Excel workbook by clicking the "Close & Load" button in the Power Query editor.

Step 6: Save Changes

1. Save your Power Query changes by clicking the "Apply & Close" button. This ensures that the grouping and aggregation rules are preserved as part of your Power BI or Excel project.

Illustrative Examples:

Here are examples to illustrate data grouping in Power Query:

Example 1 - Grouping Sales Data by Product Category:

1. In the Power Query editor, select your sales data query.

2. Click on "Group By" and choose "Product Category" as the grouping criterion.

3. Apply the aggregate function "Sum" to calculate the total sales for each product category.

Example 2 - Nested Grouping by Region and Month:

1. Select the sales data query in the Power Query editor.

2. Click on "Group By" and choose "Region" as the first grouping criterion.

3. Then, within the same "Group By" dialog, choose "Month" as the second grouping criterion.

4. Apply aggregate functions like "Sum" and "Count" to calculate sales totals and transaction counts for each region-month combination.

Conclusion:

Data grouping in Power Query is a powerful technique for organizing and analyzing data effectively. By following these steps, you can create structured summaries, gain insights within specific groups, and enhance your data manipulation skills for analysis and reporting in Power BI and Excel.

6.2 Aggregating Data

In this section, we will explore the essential skill of aggregating data using Power Query. Aggregation allows you to summarize and analyze data by performing calculations on groups or subsets of your dataset. Whether you need to calculate totals, averages, or other statistics, aggregating data is a fundamental technique for data analysis. This chapter provides a detailed guide on how to aggregate data effectively and includes practical examples for a better understanding.

Understanding Data Aggregation:

Data aggregation involves combining and summarizing values within your dataset, typically to obtain meaningful statistics. When you aggregate data, you create a condensed view that simplifies the information you're working with. Here are key concepts related to data aggregation in Power Query:

1. Aggregation Functions: You use aggregate functions to perform calculations on your data, such as sum, count, average, max, or min. These functions operate on specific columns or groups of data.

2. Grouping and Aggregation: Often, data aggregation is performed in conjunction with data grouping. You group data by one or more criteria and then apply aggregate functions to each group.

3. Custom Aggregation: Power Query allows you to create custom aggregate functions to perform more specialized calculations.

4. Resulting Data: After aggregation, you obtain summary views or tables that provide insights into the dataset, such as total sales, average prices, or maximum values.

Implementing Data Aggregation in Power Query:

Here is a step-by-step process to implement data aggregation in Power Query:

Step 1: Select Data for Aggregation

1. Open the Power Query editor in Power BI or Excel and load the dataset you want to work with.

2. In the Power Query editor, select the query containing the data you want to aggregate.

Step 2: Choose Aggregation Functions

1. In the Power Query editor, select the column or columns for which you want to perform data aggregation.

2. Click on the "Group By" option, typically found in the "Home" or "Transform" tab.

3. Choose the aggregate functions you need, such as sum, count, average, max, or min, for the selected columns.

Step 3: Review and Transform Data

1. Review the aggregated data in the Power Query Editor to ensure that the calculations meet your requirements.

2. Further transform the aggregated data, such as renaming columns, changing data types, or applying additional transformations.

Step 4: Load Data

1. Once you're satisfied with the aggregated dataset, load it into your Power BI or Excel workbook using the "Close & Load" button.

Step 5: Save Changes

1. Save your Power Query changes to preserve the aggregation rules as part of your project.

Illustrative Examples:

Here are examples to illustrate data aggregation in Power Query:

Example 1 - Aggregating Sales Data:

1. In the Power Query editor, select your sales data query.

2. Click on "Group By" and choose the "Product Category" column as the grouping criterion.

3. Apply the aggregate function "Sum" to calculate total sales within each product category.

Example 2 - Custom Aggregation for Customer Data:

1. Select your customer data query in the Power Query editor.

2. Click on "Group By" and choose the "Age" column as the grouping criterion.

3. Create a custom aggregate function to calculate the average income for each age group.

Conclusion:

Data aggregation is a fundamental technique for summarizing and analyzing data in Power Query. By following these steps and examples, you can gain deeper insights, create meaningful summaries, and enhance your data manipulation skills for analysis and reporting in Power BI and Excel.

6.3 Pivoting and Unpivoting Data

In this section, we delve into the powerful capabilities of pivoting and unpivoting data using Power Query. These techniques are essential for transforming data from a wide format to a long format (and vice versa) to suit your analysis or reporting needs. Pivoting helps you transpose data, making it more structured, while unpivoting allows you to convert data from a summarized format into a more detailed view. This chapter provides a comprehensive guide on pivoting and unpivoting data with practical examples for clarity.

Understanding Pivoting and Unpivoting:

1. Pivoting Data: Pivoting is the process of changing the structure of your data, typically from a "wide" format to a "long" format. It involves converting column headers into rows to create a more structured dataset for analysis.

2. Unpivoting Data: Unpivoting is the reverse operation of pivoting. It transforms data from a summarized format (long) into a more detailed view (wide) by combining rows into columns.

3. Use Cases: Pivoting is often used when dealing with data captured in crosstab format, like a pivot table, where you want to convert row labels into columns. Unpivoting is useful when you have data in an aggregated or summarized format and need to return it to its original detailed form for analysis.

Implementing Pivoting and Unpivoting in Power Query:

Here is a step-by-step process for implementing pivoting and unpivoting in Power Query:

Pivoting Data:

1. In the Power Query editor, select the query that contains the data you want to pivot.

2. Select the columns you want to pivot and use the "Pivot Column" option. Specify the values to aggregate, column headers, and the aggregation function if needed.

3. Review and transform the pivoted data, making any necessary adjustments to column names, data types, or additional transformations.

4. Load the pivoted data into your Power BI or Excel workbook.

Unpivoting Data:

1. In the Power Query editor, select the query that contains the data you want to unpivot.

2. Choose the columns you want to unpivot, and use the "Unpivot Columns" option. Configure the column name and data column.

3. Review and transform the unpivoted data as required.

4. Load the unpivoted data into your Power BI or Excel workbook.

Illustrative Examples:

Here are examples to illustrate pivoting and unpivoting in Power Query:

Example 1 - Pivoting Sales Data:

1. In the Power Query editor, select your sales data query with a "Product" column and monthly sales columns.

2. Use the "Pivot Column" option to pivot the monthly sales columns into rows, using "Product" as the key column.

Example 2 - Unpivoting Survey Data:

1. Select your survey data query with columns for questions and responses.

2. Apply "Unpivot Columns" to convert the responses into a long format.

Conclusion:

Pivoting and unpivoting data in Power Query are vital techniques for reshaping and structuring your data to better suit your analytical needs. By following these steps and examples, you can efficiently pivot and unpivot your data, making it more accessible and ready for analysis in Power BI and Excel.

CHAPTER III
Power Query in Real-World Scenarios

Part 7. Power Query in Excel: Tips and Tricks

7.1 Data Preparation for Excel Reports

In this chapter, we will explore the essential techniques and best practices for effectively preparing data in Power Query to create insightful Excel reports. Data preparation is a critical step in the data analysis process, and using Power Query in Excel can significantly streamline this process. We will cover various aspects of data preparation, including data cleaning, structuring, and transformation, with a focus on real-world scenarios.

Key Aspects of Data Preparation:

1. Data Cleaning: The first step in data preparation is cleaning the data. This involves identifying and handling missing values, removing duplicates, correcting data types, and addressing any data quality issues.

2. Data Structuring: Structuring the data involves organizing it in a way that is conducive to analysis. This may include pivoting, unpivoting, and reshaping the data to fit your reporting requirements.

3. Data Transformation: Data often requires transformation to create calculated columns, derive new variables, or apply custom business logic. Power Query provides a range of transformation options, such as merging queries, grouping, and aggregating.

Practical Tips and Tricks:

1. Automating Data Refresh: Learn how to set up automatic data refresh in Excel using Power Query. This ensures that your reports stay up to date without manual intervention.

2. Parameterized Queries: Explore the use of parameters to create flexible queries that allow users to customize data retrieval based on their specific needs.

3. Advanced Data Modeling: Discover advanced data modeling techniques in Power Query, including creating relationships between tables and using DAX functions to enhance data analysis.

Real-World Scenario Example: Data Cleaning and Transformation

Suppose you have a dataset with sales data, and it contains missing values and inconsistent date formats. Here's how you can prepare the data using Power Query:

1. Data Cleaning:

  - Remove rows with missing values or replace them with meaningful data.

  - Standardize date formats to ensure consistency.

2. Data Structuring:

  - Pivot the data to create a summary view for reporting.

- Unpivot the data to create a detailed view for analysis.

3. Data Transformation:

  - Calculate new columns, such as profit margins or sales growth.

  - Merge the sales data with customer information from another data source.

By following these steps and applying the practical tips and tricks mentioned in this chapter, you can efficiently prepare your data for Excel reports, ensuring that your reports are accurate and up-to-date.

Conclusion:

Data preparation is a fundamental part of data analysis, and Power Query in Excel offers powerful tools and techniques to streamline this process. This chapter equips you with the knowledge and skills to prepare data effectively for Excel reports, making your analysis and reporting tasks more efficient and accurate.

7.2 Automating Data Refresh

In this chapter, we delve into the critical aspect of automating data refresh in Excel using Power Query. Automating data refresh is essential for maintaining the accuracy and relevance of your reports without the need for manual intervention. Whether your data sources are regularly updated databases, web services, or external files, Power Query provides the tools to streamline the data refresh process. We will explore the key concepts and practical steps to automate data refresh efficiently.

Key Concepts for Automating Data Refresh:

1. Connection Settings: Ensure that your Power Query connections are configured to enable automatic data refresh. Verify the connection details, such as the source location and authentication settings.

2. Scheduled Refresh: Excel allows you to schedule data refresh at specific intervals, such as daily, weekly, or monthly. Set up a refresh schedule that aligns with your data source's update frequency.

3. Data Source Options: Depending on the data source, you may need to configure specific data source options. For example, for databases, set up connection parameters, or for web services, define authentication tokens.

Practical Steps to Automate Data Refresh:

1. Configuring Data Connection:

   - Open your Excel workbook that contains the Power Query queries.

   - Navigate to the "Data" tab and choose "Connections."

   - Select the connection that you want to refresh automatically and click "Properties."

   - In the "Connection Properties" dialog, go to the "Usage" tab, where you can configure refresh options.

2. Scheduled Refresh:

   - In the "Connection Properties" dialog, go to the "Usage" tab, where you can set the refresh frequency. Choose the desired refresh frequency, such as daily or weekly.

   - Specify the time of day when the refresh should occur.

3. Data Source Options:

- For specific data sources, ensure that you have set up the necessary credentials and connection parameters. Power Query will use these settings during automated refresh.

Real-World Scenario Example: Automated Database Refresh

Suppose you have an Excel report that relies on a database as its data source, and the database is regularly updated with new sales data. To automate data refresh:

1. Connection Configuration:

   - Configure the database connection in Power Query with the necessary server and database information.

   - Set up authentication details, such as a username and password, and save them securely.

2. Scheduled Refresh:

   - Schedule a daily refresh of the database connection. This ensures that the Excel report always reflects the most up-to-date sales data.

By following these steps, your Excel report will automatically refresh the data from the database daily, ensuring that your reports are always current without manual intervention.

Conclusion:

Automating data refresh in Excel with Power Query is a powerful feature that enhances the efficiency and accuracy of your reporting process. This chapter provides the guidance and practical steps needed to configure and schedule data refresh, making your Excel reports reliable and up-to-date.

7.3 Advanced Data Modeling in Excel

In this chapter, we will explore the advanced data modeling capabilities of Power Query in Excel. While Power Query is renowned for its data transformation and preparation features, it also provides powerful tools for creating sophisticated data models that enhance your reporting and analysis. We will delve into the following key aspects of advanced data modeling:

Key Concepts for Advanced Data Modeling:

1. Relationships: Understand the concept of establishing relationships between tables in your data model. Relationships allow you to combine data from multiple sources and create meaningful connections between them.

2. Calculated Columns: Learn how to create calculated columns in your data model. Calculated columns enable you to add custom calculations or derive new information based on existing data.

3. Measures and DAX: Dive into Data Analysis Expressions (DAX) and how it can be used to create measures. Measures are essential for performing aggregations and calculations across your data model.

4. Hierarchies: Explore the creation of hierarchies within your data model. Hierarchies provide a structured way to navigate and drill down into data for deeper insights.

Practical Steps for Advanced Data Modeling:

1. Establishing Relationships:

   - Identify common fields in multiple tables that can serve as the basis for relationships.

   - Use the "Diagram View" in Power Query to visually define relationships between tables.

- Choose the type of relationship, such as one-to-one or one-to-many, based on your data structure.

2. Calculated Columns:

- Define calculated columns by creating custom formulas. For example, you can create a calculated column that calculates the profit margin based on revenue and cost data.

- Utilize DAX functions within calculated columns to perform complex calculations.

3. Measures and DAX:

- Write DAX expressions to create measures that aggregate data or perform calculations, such as sum, average, or year-over-year growth.

- Use DAX functions like SUMX, AVERAGE, or CALCULATE to build powerful measures.

4. Hierarchies:

- Create hierarchies by organizing data attributes in a structured manner. For example, you can create a time hierarchy with levels for year, quarter, and month.

- Hierarchies enable more intuitive data exploration and analysis.

Real-World Scenario Example: Sales Data Analysis

Imagine you have a data model with tables for sales transactions, products, and customers. To perform advanced data modeling:

1. Establishing Relationships:

- Establish relationships between the sales transactions and products and between the sales transactions and customers based on common keys.

2. Calculated Columns:

   - Create a calculated column that computes the profit margin for each transaction by subtracting the cost from the revenue.

3. Measures and DAX:

   - Develop DAX measures for total sales, average order value, and year-over-year sales growth.

4. Hierarchies:

   - Construct a time hierarchy with levels for year, quarter, and month for more in-depth time-based analysis.

By implementing these advanced data modeling techniques, you can gain deeper insights and provide more meaningful reports and dashboards to your users.

Conclusion:

Advanced data modeling in Excel with Power Query empowers you to create sophisticated data models, build relationships, define calculated columns, and use DAX expressions to perform complex calculations. This chapter equips you with the knowledge and tools to take your data modeling to the next level, enhancing the depth and quality of your data analysis and reporting.

Part 8. Power Query in Power BI: Data Transformation and Modeling

8.1 Data Preparation for Power BI Reports

In this chapter, we will explore the critical role of data preparation for creating effective Power BI reports. Data preparation is the foundation for successful data modeling, visualization, and decision-making in Power BI. We will focus on key aspects of data preparation to ensure your Power BI reports are insightful and accurate.

The Importance of Data Preparation:

Data preparation is the initial phase in the Power BI development process. It involves cleaning, transforming, and structuring your data to make it suitable for analysis and visualization. Effective data preparation ensures that your Power BI reports provide accurate and reliable insights.

Key Steps in Data Preparation:

1. Data Source Connection: Begin by connecting to your data sources. Power BI allows you to connect to a wide range of sources, including databases, Excel files, web services, and more.

2. Data Loading: Load your data into Power BI using Power Query. Power Query provides a user-friendly interface for cleaning and transforming data.

3. Data Cleaning: Clean your data by addressing issues like missing values, duplicate records, and data outliers. Power Query offers a set of data cleaning tools to assist in this process.

4. Data Transformation: Transform your data to meet the specific requirements of your analysis. This includes tasks like renaming columns, creating calculated columns, and aggregating data.

5. Data Modeling: Create relationships between different tables in your data model. Power BI's data modeling capabilities allow you to define relationships, calculated tables, and measures.

Practical Example: Sales Data Analysis

Let's consider a practical example where you need to prepare sales data for a Power BI report:

1. Data Source Connection: Connect to your sales database, which contains transaction records, customer information, and product data.

2. Data Loading: Use Power Query to load the data into Power BI.

3. Data Cleaning: Address issues like missing customer information and remove duplicate transactions.

4. Data Transformation: Create calculated columns, such as profit margin, and aggregate data for reporting.

5. Data Modeling: Define relationships between the sales, customer, and product tables to enable meaningful analysis.

Conclusion:

Data preparation is a fundamental step in creating successful Power BI reports. It ensures that your data is accurate, structured, and ready for analysis. By following the key steps outlined in this chapter and applying them to real-world scenarios, you can significantly enhance the quality and effectiveness of your Power BI reports. Effective data preparation is the cornerstone of insightful data visualization and decision-making.

8.2 Using Power Query in Power BI Desktop

In this chapter, we will dive into the practical aspects of using Power Query within Power BI Desktop. Power Query is a powerful data transformation and preparation tool integrated into Power BI, allowing you to shape your data before building reports and visualizations. We'll explore how to use Power Query effectively to connect, transform, and model data for your Power BI reports.

Key Aspects of Using Power Query in Power BI Desktop:

1. Connecting to Data Sources: Power BI Desktop provides a user-friendly interface for connecting to various data sources, including databases, Excel files, cloud services, and web sources. We'll walk you through the process of establishing connections to extract data.

2. Accessing Power Query Editor: Learn how to access Power Query Editor within Power BI Desktop, where you can view and modify the data transformation steps. We'll explore the different transformation options available.

3. Data Transformation: Understand how to clean, reshape, and combine data using the Power Query editor. You'll see practical examples of tasks like removing columns, filtering rows, and merging queries.

4. Data Loading: Explore the options for loading data into your Power BI data model. We'll discuss the implications of data load options on performance and report responsiveness.

Practical Example: Sales Data Transformation

Let's consider a real-world scenario where you have sales data from different regions and sources, and you want to use Power Query within Power BI Desktop:

1. Connecting to Data: We'll demonstrate how to connect to multiple data sources, such as Excel spreadsheets and a cloud-based CRM system, and consolidate the data within Power Query.

2. Data Transformation: You'll see how to clean and transform the data, including removing unnecessary columns, filtering out irrelevant records, and standardizing date formats.

3. Data Integration: Learn how to combine data from various sources into a unified dataset, which can serve as the foundation for your Power BI reports.

4. Data Loading: Understand the options for loading the transformed data into Power BI and the implications for data refresh and report performance.

Benefits of Effective Data Transformation:

Using Power Query within Power BI Desktop provides you with the ability to create clean, structured, and well-modeled data, which is essential for generating meaningful insights and interactive reports. Effective data transformation enhances the overall data visualization and analysis experience in Power BI.

By following the guidance and examples in this chapter, you'll be equipped with the practical knowledge needed to harness the full potential of Power Query in Power BI Desktop, enabling you to build impactful reports and dashboards with confidence.

8.3 Managing Dataflows and Data Refresh

In this chapter, we'll explore the critical aspects of managing dataflows and ensuring the timely and accurate data refresh in Power BI. Dataflows play a pivotal role in creating a structured and streamlined data preparation process, while efficient data refresh mechanisms guarantee that your reports and visualizations are always up to date.

Key Considerations for Managing Dataflows and Data Refresh:

1. Understanding Dataflows: We'll begin by explaining the concept of dataflows in Power BI. Dataflows allow you to create reusable, standardized ETL (Extract, Transform, Load) processes that can be shared across multiple reports.

2. Creating Dataflows: Learn how to create, configure, and maintain dataflows within Power BI. This involves defining data source connections, transformations, and data storage settings.

3. Dataflow Dependencies: Understand the relationships between dataflows and their dependencies. We'll illustrate how different dataflows can rely on one another, creating a network of interconnected data preparation processes.

4. Data Refresh Scheduling: Explore the options for scheduling data refreshes, ensuring that your dataflows stay up to date with the source systems. We'll discuss considerations for selecting appropriate refresh frequencies.

5. Dataflow Optimization: Discover techniques for optimizing dataflows to minimize resource consumption and enhance overall performance.

Practical Example: Sales Data Management with Dataflows

To illustrate the concepts covered in this chapter, let's consider a real-world scenario:

Scenario: You have a complex data landscape with sales data coming from various sources, including Excel files, on-premises databases, and cloud-based systems. You need to create dataflows to streamline the data preparation process and ensure that your Power BI reports reflect the most current sales data.

Steps:

1. Creating Dataflows: We'll guide you through the process of creating separate dataflows for different data sources. You'll set up transformations to clean and harmonize the data.

2. Managing Dependencies: Learn how to establish dependencies between dataflows. For instance, dataflow A may depend on the output of dataflow B, and we'll show how to configure these relationships.

3. Data Refresh Scheduling: Explore the scheduling options for refreshing dataflows. You'll decide on the refresh frequency that best suits your organization's needs.

4. Optimizing Dataflows: We'll provide tips for optimizing your dataflows to minimize storage and processing overhead while maximizing performance.

By following our guidance and real-world examples, you'll gain a comprehensive understanding of how to efficiently manage dataflows and data refresh in Power BI. This knowledge will empower you to create well-structured, automated data preparation workflows, ensuring that your Power BI reports consistently provide valuable insights based on the most current data.

Part 9. Case Studies and Practical Examples

9.1 Sales Analysis: Combining Data from Multiple Sources

In this section, we delve into a comprehensive case study that demonstrates the power of Power Query in transforming and shaping data for sales analysis. You'll encounter a real-world scenario where sales data is scattered across multiple sources, such as Excel spreadsheets, CRM systems, and cloud-based databases. The objective is to consolidate this disparate data and create a cohesive analysis for better decision-making.

Scenario Overview:

Imagine you work for a retail company with a vast sales operation. Sales data is generated daily from various touchpoints, including physical stores, e-commerce platforms, and third-party sales channels. The data is stored in Excel files, a CRM system, and a cloud database. To gain a comprehensive view of sales performance, you need to merge and transform this data into a unified dataset.

Key Steps in the Case Study:

1. Data Source Identification: We'll guide you through the process of identifying and accessing the various data sources, highlighting the importance of understanding data structure and quality.

2. Data Extraction: Learn how to extract data from the different sources using Power Query. This involves connecting to Excel files, CRM systems, and cloud databases.

3. Data Transformation: Discover the techniques to clean, transform, and harmonize the data. We'll address issues like data type conversions, handling missing values, and merging data from multiple sources.

4. Data Consolidation: Understand how to append and merge data tables to create a consolidated dataset suitable for sales analysis.

5. Creating a Sales Dashboard: Once your data is prepared, we'll briefly introduce you to the process of building a sales dashboard in Power BI to visualize the insights gained from the merged data.

Practical Example: Combining Sales Data

To provide a glimpse into the case study, let's consider one specific example:

Example: You have sales data in Excel spreadsheets, CRM records, and a cloud-based database. In the Excel files, the data is stored in multiple sheets, each representing different product categories. Your task is to consolidate data from all these sources to evaluate sales performance across various product categories over a specific timeframe.

Steps:

1. Data Source Connection: We'll walk you through connecting to the Excel files, CRM system, and cloud database using Power Query.

2. Data Extraction: You'll learn how to extract relevant data from these sources while addressing issues like data format discrepancies.

3. Data Transformation: We'll cover data transformations, including merging data from different product category sheets, standardizing data types, and handling any discrepancies.

4. Data Consolidation: Discover how to consolidate the transformed data into a single table for analysis.

By following this case study and practical example, you'll gain hands-on experience in combining and analyzing data from various sources for sales analysis. The skills acquired will empower you to apply the same principles to similar scenarios within your organization, unlocking valuable insights and improving decision-making processes.

9.2 Financial Reporting: Budget vs. Actuals

In this section, we explore a practical case study that demonstrates how Power Query can be employed to streamline financial reporting by comparing budgeted figures with actual results. Financial reporting is a critical aspect of any organization, and the ability to efficiently analyze, transform, and visualize financial data is paramount for effective decision-making.

Scenario Overview:

Imagine you are a financial analyst in a medium-sized company responsible for creating periodic financial reports. Your company maintains separate records for budgeted and actual financial data, typically stored in Excel spreadsheets or accounting software. Your task is to use Power Query to automate the process of comparing budgeted figures with actual results, identifying variances, and producing comprehensive financial reports.

Key Steps in the Case Study:

1. Data Source Identification: We will guide you through identifying and accessing the budgeted and actual financial data sources, emphasizing the importance of data quality and consistency.

2. Data Extraction: Learn how to extract financial data from the budget and actual sources, which may include Excel spreadsheets, accounting software exports, or databases.

3. Data Transformation: Discover techniques to cleanse and shape the data, ensuring that it's consistent and ready for analysis. This includes dealing with differences in data structure, handling missing data, and aligning data types.

4. Combining Data: Use Power Query to merge the budgeted and actual data, aligning them for direct comparison.

5. Calculating Variances: Learn how to create calculated columns or measures to compute variances between budgeted and actual figures.

6. Creating Financial Reports: Utilize Power Query and Power BI to produce financial reports and interactive dashboards that provide insights into budget vs. actual performance.

Practical Example: Comparing Budget vs. Actuals

As a glimpse into the case study, let's consider a specific example:

Example: You have budgeted financial data stored in an Excel spreadsheet, and actual financial results exported from accounting software. Your goal is to automate the process of comparing budgeted revenues with actual revenues for the current fiscal year.

Steps:

1. Data Source Connection: We'll guide you through connecting to the Excel budget file and the exported actual financial data using Power Query.

2. Data Extraction: Learn how to extract relevant financial data from these sources while addressing potential discrepancies in data structure.

3. Data Transformation: We'll cover data transformations, including standardizing data types, dealing with missing data, and aligning data structure for consistent comparison.

4. Data Combining: Discover how to merge the budgeted and actual data, aligning them for accurate budget vs. actual analysis.

5. Calculating Variances: Learn how to create calculated columns or measures in Power BI to compute variances and visualize the results.

By following this case study and practical example, you'll gain hands-on experience in automating financial reporting processes and efficiently comparing budgeted figures with actual results. These skills will empower you to enhance financial analysis and reporting within your organization, ultimately facilitating better financial decision-making.

9.3 Marketing Analytics: Campaign Performance

In this section, we delve into a real-world case study that showcases how Power Query can be leveraged to optimize marketing analytics by assessing the performance of various marketing campaigns. Marketing analytics is a critical practice for businesses aiming to gauge the effectiveness of their marketing efforts, allocate resources efficiently, and fine-tune their strategies.

Scenario Overview:

Imagine you are a marketing manager in a growing e-commerce company that runs multiple marketing campaigns across various platforms, such as social media, email marketing, and search engine advertising. Your objective is to employ Power Query to automate the process of gathering data from these campaigns, analyzing their performance, and producing comprehensive reports.

Key Steps in the Case Study:

1. Data Collection: We'll guide you through the process of collecting data from diverse marketing sources, emphasizing the significance of consistent data structures and quality.

2. Data Extraction: Learn how to extract marketing data from different platforms, including data sources like Google Analytics, Facebook Ads, and email marketing platforms.

3. Data Transformation: Discover techniques to cleanse and format the data for analysis. This includes handling data inconsistencies, data type conversion, and preparing the data for merging.

4. Data Integration: Use Power Query to combine data from multiple marketing campaigns into a unified dataset for in-depth analysis.

5. Performance Metrics: Understand how to calculate and analyze key marketing performance metrics, such as click-through rates, conversion rates, return on investment (ROI), and customer acquisition cost (CAC).

6. Data Visualization: Learn how to create compelling visualizations and dashboards to provide insights into the performance of each marketing campaign.

Practical Example: Analyzing Campaign Performance

As a practical illustration, let's consider a specific example:

Example: Your e-commerce company runs advertising campaigns on Facebook and Google Ads. Your goal is to assess the performance of these campaigns for a specific period and determine which one yields a higher return on ad spend (ROAS).

Steps:

1. Data Collection: We will demonstrate how to gather data from Facebook Ads and Google Ads through Power Query, ensuring data consistency.

2. Data Extraction: Learn how to extract relevant campaign data, including impressions, clicks, costs, and conversion data.

3. Data Transformation: We'll cover data cleansing and data type standardization, preparing the data for comparison.

4. Data Integration: Use Power Query to merge data from both advertising platforms into a cohesive dataset.

5. Performance Metrics: Calculate the ROAS for each campaign and assess which one is more effective in terms of advertising ROI.

6. Data Visualization: Create interactive dashboards in Power BI to visualize campaign performance, providing actionable insights for future marketing strategies.

By following this case study and practical example, you'll gain hands-on experience in automating marketing analytics processes, efficiently evaluating campaign performance, and optimizing marketing strategies. These skills will empower you to make data-driven decisions, allocate resources effectively, and enhance the success of your marketing efforts.

CHAPTER IV
Power Query Best Practices and Optimization

Part 10. Power Query Performance Optimization

10.1 Query Folding and Pushdown

In this chapter, we will delve into the crucial aspects of optimizing Power Query performance, with a specific focus on query folding and pushdown. These techniques are paramount to ensure that your data transformation processes are as efficient and expedient as possible, resulting in reduced data refresh times and enhanced resource management.

Understanding Query Folding:

Query folding is a technique employed by Power Query to enhance the performance of your data transformations. It is based on the concept of pushing as much of the data processing work as possible back to the data source. When you apply transformations in Power Query, the software attempts to convert these operations into native queries that can be executed by the data source itself. This approach significantly reduces the volume of data that needs to be loaded into memory, thereby improving both processing speed and resource efficiency.

Key Considerations and Techniques for Query Folding:

1. Source Compatibility: Query folding is most effective when your data source supports it. Common data sources such as relational databases, online services, and cloud-based data warehouses often provide robust support for query folding.

2. Step Sequencing: The order in which you apply transformations in Power Query can impact the potential for query folding. Understanding the sequence of steps and the logic applied is essential to achieve maximum optimization.

3. Connector-Level Implementation: Some Power Query connectors, such as the OLE DB or ODBC connectors, offer robust query folding capabilities. Leveraging these connectors when connecting to compatible data sources is recommended.

Practical Example:

Let's consider an example to illustrate the significance of query folding:

Example: You have a large dataset stored in a SQL Server database, and you need to filter the data to include only records from the year 2022. Instead of loading the entire dataset into Power Query and then applying the filter, you can utilize query folding. By directly pushing the filter operation to the SQL Server database, it will retrieve only the relevant data, reducing data transfer and memory consumption.

Steps:

1. Data Source Connection: Connect to your SQL Server database using Power Query.

2. Filter Operation: Apply a filter to retrieve records for the year 2022.

3. Query Folding: Power Query will recognize the filter operation as a native SQL query that can be executed by the database server. The filtering process occurs at the source, reducing the data load into Power Query.

By implementing query folding in this manner, you minimize resource usage, enhance query performance, and optimize your data transformation processes.

Conclusion:

Understanding and applying query folding techniques is instrumental in improving Power Query performance. By pushing as much of the processing work as possible back to the data source, you can significantly reduce data refresh times and better manage memory and resources. Mastering these techniques will empower you to work with large datasets efficiently and ensure that your data transformation tasks run smoothly and expediently.

10.2 Reducing Data Refresh Time

This chapter is dedicated to the art of optimizing your Power Query solutions to minimize data refresh time. In the realm of data transformation and modeling, efficiency is key. Reducing data refresh time not only makes your reports and dashboards more responsive but also lessens the strain on your system resources, ultimately leading to a more productive and reliable Power Query experience.

Understanding the Significance of Data Refresh Time:

Data refresh time refers to the duration it takes to update the data in your Power Query solution. When working with large datasets or complex transformations, data refresh can be a time-consuming process. By optimizing this aspect, you can make your Power Query-based reports and models more agile.

Key Strategies to Reduce Data Refresh Time:

1. Query Folding: As discussed in the previous section, leveraging query folding is fundamental in reducing data refresh time. This technique offloads as much processing work as possible to the data source, limiting the amount of data transferred and processed in Power Query.

2. Filtering and Extraction: Minimize the data you pull into Power Query by employing filtering techniques. Retrieve only the data you need for your reports, reducing the dataset size and accelerating refresh times.

3. Data Source Indexing: Ensure that your data sources are appropriately indexed to facilitate faster data retrieval. Well-indexed data sources significantly expedite the data refresh process.

Practical Example:

Let's consider an example to elucidate the concept of reducing data refresh time:

Example: You're working with a financial dataset for a large organization. The dataset contains years of financial records, but your report focuses on the current fiscal year only. Rather than refreshing all the historical data with each update, you can use data filtering to extract and load only the current fiscal year's data. This approach significantly reduces data refresh time and optimizes resource usage.

Steps:

1. Data Extraction: Configure your Power Query solution to extract data for the current fiscal year only.

2. Data Refresh: When you refresh your report or model, only the relevant data for the current fiscal year is retrieved and processed.

By employing this method, you not only streamline data refresh but also enhance report responsiveness, especially when dealing with extensive historical data.

Conclusion:

Reducing data refresh time is a vital aspect of Power Query performance optimization. By focusing on techniques such as query folding, data filtering, and efficient data source indexing, you can significantly enhance the efficiency of your Power Query-based solutions. A well-optimized Power Query environment results in faster report updates, better resource management, and ultimately, a more efficient data transformation process. Mastering these techniques will empower you to create responsive and resource-efficient Power Query solutions.

10.3 Memory Management and Resource Usage

In this chapter, we delve into the critical aspect of memory management and resource usage within Power Query. Understanding how Power Query handles memory and system resources is essential to ensure the efficient functioning of your data transformation processes. By optimizing memory usage and resource allocation, you can avoid bottlenecks and enhance the overall performance of your Power Query solutions.

The Significance of Memory Management and Resource Usage:

Power Query operates within the constraints of your computer's memory and resources. The efficient utilization of memory is crucial, especially when dealing with large datasets and complex transformations. By managing memory effectively, you can prevent performance issues and system crashes.

Key Strategies for Memory Management and Resource Usage:

1. Data Reduction: Minimize the amount of data loaded into memory by using filtering, column removal, and other techniques. Loading only the necessary data reduces memory usage and speeds up processing.

2. Data Type Optimization: Ensure that data types are selected appropriately. Using more memory-efficient data types (e.g., Integer instead of Decimal) can conserve resources.

3. Resource Monitoring: Keep an eye on system resource utilization while refreshing your queries. Tools like the Windows Task Manager or Performance Monitor can help identify resource-heavy processes.

Practical Example:

Let's consider an example to illustrate the importance of memory management and resource usage:

Example: You are working on a project involving a large dataset of customer orders. During data refresh, your system frequently runs into memory-related performance issues. To address this, you decide to optimize memory usage.

Steps:

1. Data Reduction: You apply filtering to load only orders from the current year, reducing the dataset's size.

2. Data Type Optimization: You review the data types and discover that some columns use excessively large data types. For example, you change the data type for the "Discount" column from Decimal to Percentage, which conserves memory.

3. Resource Monitoring: During query refresh, you monitor system resource usage. By observing the memory consumption and CPU utilization, you identify opportunities to further optimize the process.

By optimizing memory management and resource usage, you not only prevent performance bottlenecks but also ensure a smoother and more efficient Power Query experience.

Conclusion:

Efficient memory management and resource usage are paramount in Power Query performance optimization. By implementing strategies such as data reduction, data type optimization, and resource monitoring, you can optimize memory usage and resource allocation. This leads to faster data transformations, smoother data refresh processes, and ultimately, a more efficient Power Query environment. Mastering these techniques is essential for creating responsive and reliable data transformation solutions.

Part 11. Data Governance and Security

11.1 Data Privacy and Security Settings

Data privacy and security are paramount in any data transformation and analytics process. In this chapter, we explore the critical aspects of managing data privacy and security settings in Power Query to ensure the confidentiality and integrity of your data.

Understanding Data Privacy and Security Settings:

Data privacy and security settings in Power Query allow you to control how data is accessed and handled during the data transformation process. It is crucial to safeguard sensitive information and comply with regulatory requirements.

Key Concepts in Data Privacy and Security:

1. Data Source Credentials: Power Query enables you to specify credentials for data sources. For instance, you can configure username and password authentication for a database connection. It's essential to choose the appropriate authentication method and protect these credentials.

2. Privacy Levels: Power Query assigns privacy levels to data sources to determine their interaction. High privacy levels restrict data sharing between sources to prevent unintended data leaks. Understanding and configuring privacy levels are vital for secure data handling.

3. Data Encryption: Utilize encryption protocols when connecting to secure data sources. Ensure that data transmission between your data source and Power Query is encrypted to protect data in transit.

4. Query Folding: Query folding is a technique that pushes data transformation tasks back to the data source, minimizing data exposure in Power Query. Leveraging query folding enhances data security by reducing the amount of sensitive data transferred to Power Query.

Practical Example:

Let's consider an example to illustrate the significance of data privacy and security settings:

Example: You are working with a financial dataset containing sensitive customer information. It is crucial to maintain data privacy and security during data transformations.

Steps:

1. Data Source Credentials: Configure secure access to the financial database with appropriate credentials, such as username and password, ensuring access control.

2. Privacy Levels: Set privacy levels for the financial database and other data sources. Define strict privacy levels to limit data sharing between sources, preventing sensitive data from combining with less sensitive data.

3. Data Encryption: Ensure that data transmission from the financial database to Power Query is encrypted, preventing data interception during transit.

4. Query Folding: Leverage query folding techniques to push data transformation operations back to the financial database whenever possible. This minimizes the exposure of sensitive data within Power Query.

By implementing robust data privacy and security settings, you protect sensitive information, comply with data protection regulations, and maintain the confidentiality and integrity of your data.

Conclusion:

Data privacy and security settings play a critical role in ensuring the confidentiality and integrity of data during the data transformation process. By understanding and applying concepts like data source credentials, privacy levels, data encryption, and query folding, you can safeguard sensitive information and mitigate data security risks. Mastering these techniques is essential for achieving robust data governance and security practices in Power Query.

11.2 Data Classification and Sensitivity Labels

Data classification and sensitivity labels are essential components of a comprehensive data governance and security strategy. In this chapter, we delve into the significance of data classification and sensitivity labels in Power Query for ensuring data confidentiality and regulatory compliance.

Understanding Data Classification and Sensitivity Labels:

Data classification is the process of categorizing data based on its importance, sensitivity, and regulatory requirements. Sensitivity labels are metadata tags or labels that provide information about the sensitivity and handling requirements of data.

Key Concepts in Data Classification and Sensitivity Labels:

1. Data Categorization: Start by categorizing your data into various classes based on its importance and sensitivity. For example, you can classify data as "public," "confidential," or "restricted."

2. Sensitivity Labels: Sensitivity labels are attached to data sources, datasets, or specific columns. These labels convey the data's sensitivity level and any restrictions or handling requirements.

3. Handling Requirements: Define the handling requirements for data with sensitivity labels. For instance, "confidential" data may have restrictions on sharing, while "public" data can be freely shared.

4. Regulatory Compliance: Data sensitivity labels aid in compliance with data protection regulations, such as GDPR or HIPAA, by ensuring that sensitive data is handled appropriately.

Practical Example:

Let's consider an example to illustrate the importance of data classification and sensitivity labels:

Example: You are managing a healthcare dataset that contains patient information. This data is subject to strict regulatory compliance requirements.

Steps:

1. Data Categorization: Categorize the data into "patient information" and "administrative records." "Patient information" is highly sensitive, while "administrative records" are less sensitive.

2. Sensitivity Labels: Attach sensitivity labels to the "patient information" dataset, specifying it as "confidential" and subject to strict access controls. The "administrative records" dataset can be labeled as "public."

3. Handling Requirements: Set specific handling requirements for the "confidential" dataset. Define who can access it, restrict sharing, and ensure data protection measures are in place.

4. Regulatory Compliance: The use of sensitivity labels ensures compliance with healthcare data protection regulations, such as HIPAA. It demonstrates that sensitive patient information is handled with care and in line with legal requirements.

By implementing data classification and sensitivity labels, you can effectively manage and protect sensitive data, align with regulatory requirements, and maintain a robust data governance and security framework.

Conclusion:

Data classification and sensitivity labels are critical tools for managing data sensitivity, ensuring regulatory compliance, and maintaining data security. By categorizing data, attaching sensitivity labels, defining handling requirements, and complying with regulations, you can strengthen your data governance and security practices in Power Query. This ensures that sensitive data is handled appropriately and reduces the risk of data breaches and non-compliance.

Part 12. Power Query Administration and Deployment

12.1 Sharing Queries and Data Sources

Sharing queries and data sources is a crucial aspect of Power Query administration and deployment. It enables collaboration, streamlines data access, and ensures consistent data transformation across your organization. In this chapter, we will explore the best practices for sharing queries and data sources effectively.

Understanding the Importance of Sharing Queries and Data Sources:

Sharing queries and data sources is essential for the following reasons:

1. Collaboration: It facilitates collaboration among users, allowing them to work on the same data transformations and reports.

2. Consistency: Shared queries and data sources ensure that everyone uses the same standardized data, reducing discrepancies and errors.

3. Efficiency: Users can access pre-defined queries and data sources, saving time and effort in recreating the same transformations.

4. Data Governance: Sharing enables centralized control and management of queries, ensuring compliance and security.

Best Practices for Sharing Queries and Data Sources:

1. Organize Queries: Group related queries into folders and name them descriptively for easy navigation and identification.

2. Data Source Sharing: Share data sources, such as database connections, to allow users to access the same data.

3. Query Parameters: Use query parameters to make queries dynamic and reusable for different data sources or time periods.

4. Query Privacy Levels: Configure query privacy levels to control data access and sharing based on sensitivity.

5. Shared Folders: Create shared folders or directories on your network or cloud storage to host query files and data sources.

Practical Example:

Let's consider a practical scenario to illustrate the importance of sharing queries and data sources:

Example: In a company, multiple teams work on sales data analysis using Power BI. Each team has its own data source, but they all need access to a common set of standardized sales transformations.

Steps:

1. Standardized Sales Queries: The organization's Power Query team develops standardized sales queries that cover common data transformations needed by all teams.

2. Shared Data Source: A shared data source connection to the sales database is created, and data privacy levels are set based on sensitivity.

3. Shared Queries: The standardized sales queries are saved in a shared folder accessible to all teams.

4. Query Parameters: Query parameters are used to make the standardized queries dynamic, allowing teams to specify their data source or time period.

5. Access Control: Access to the shared folder and data source is controlled based on team permissions and sensitivity levels.

By sharing standardized queries and data sources, the organization ensures that all teams work with consistent, up-to-date data while maintaining control and security.

Conclusion:

Sharing queries and data sources in Power Query is a fundamental aspect of administration and deployment. It fosters collaboration, ensures data consistency, and streamlines data access while maintaining control and governance. Implementing best practices for sharing queries and data sources can enhance the efficiency and data quality of your Power Query workflows.

12.2 Setting up Data Gateway for On-Premises Data

Setting up a Data Gateway for on-premises data sources is a crucial component of Power Query administration and deployment. A Data Gateway allows Power BI or Excel to connect securely to your organization's on-premises data sources, enabling you to create reports and dashboards with real-time data. In this chapter, we will provide a detailed guide on how to set up and configure a Data Gateway for on-premises data sources.

Understanding the Importance of Data Gateway:

A Data Gateway serves as the bridge between your Power Query reports in Power BI or Excel and on-premises data sources. This is vital for the following reasons:

1. Secure Connection: It ensures a secure and encrypted connection between cloud-based Power Query services and your on-premises data sources.

2. Real-Time Data: A Data Gateway enables real-time or scheduled data refreshes for your reports and dashboards, keeping the information up-to-date.

3. Data Source Access: It allows you to access a wide range of on-premises data sources, including databases, file shares, and web services.

4. Simplified Administration: Centralized administration and monitoring of data sources and refresh schedules.

Setting up Data Gateway:

Follow these steps to set up a Data Gateway for on-premises data:

1. Download and Install: Download the Power BI Gateway or On-Premises Data Gateway, depending on your specific use case. Install the gateway software on a server or computer that has access to your on-premises data sources.

2. Configuration: Launch the gateway and sign in with your Power BI or Excel account. Configure the gateway settings, including the gateway name and recovery key for data security.

3. Data Source Configuration: Add your on-premises data sources to the gateway. These sources may include databases, files, or web services. Define the connection details for each data source.

4. Data Refresh: Set up data refresh schedules for your data sources, specifying how often the gateway should connect and retrieve data. Ensure that your data sources and firewall configurations allow these connections.

5. Testing and Monitoring: Test the connections and data refresh to verify that the gateway is functioning correctly. Monitor the gateway's performance and data refresh logs.

Practical Example:

Let's consider a practical example to illustrate the setup of a Data Gateway:

Example: A company uses Power BI for sales reporting, and their sales data resides in an on-premises SQL Server database. They need to set up a Data Gateway to ensure that their sales reports are always up-to-date.

Steps:

1. Download and Install: The company's IT department downloads and installs the Power BI Gateway on a dedicated server with access to the on-premises SQL Server database.

2. Configuration: The IT team configures the gateway, providing a unique name and recovery key to ensure secure data transmission.

3. Data Source Configuration: They add the SQL Server database as a data source, specifying the connection details and credentials.

4. Data Refresh: A scheduled data refresh is set up to occur every day, ensuring the sales data is kept current.

5. Testing and Monitoring: The IT team tests the connection and monitors the gateway's performance using the monitoring tools provided by the gateway software.

By following these steps, the company can now create Power Query reports and dashboards in Power BI, accessing real-time data from their on-premises SQL Server database securely.

Conclusion:

Setting up a Data Gateway for on-premises data sources is essential for connecting Power Query to on-premises databases and data sources securely. By configuring and managing the Data Gateway effectively, organizations can ensure that their Power Query reports and dashboards have access to the latest on-premises data, enhancing the quality and timeliness of their analytics.

12.3 Scheduling Data Refresh

Scheduling data refresh is a fundamental aspect of Power Query administration and deployment that ensures your reports and dashboards remain updated with the latest data. Whether you're using Power BI or Excel, automating data refresh processes allows you to maintain the accuracy and relevance of your analytics. In this chapter, we'll provide detailed insights into scheduling data refresh and best practices for optimizing this critical operation.

Importance of Scheduling Data Refresh:

Scheduling data refresh is essential for various reasons:

1. Timeliness: To keep your reports and dashboards up-to-date, ensuring that users always have access to the most recent data.

2. Automation: Automating the refresh process reduces manual intervention and minimizes the risk of human errors.

3. Efficiency: Scheduling refreshes during off-peak hours or at specific intervals ensures minimal disruption to system performance.

4. Compliance: To meet business requirements and data governance policies, including regular updates and data accuracy.

Steps to Schedule Data Refresh:

1. Data Source Connection: Ensure that your data source, whether it's an on-premises database or a cloud-based service, is accessible and properly configured. Establish a reliable connection to the data source.

2. Gateway Configuration: If you are working with on-premises data sources, set up and configure a Data Gateway, as explained in section 12.2. The gateway acts as the bridge between cloud-based services and on-premises data.

3. Data Refresh Policies: Define your data refresh policies, including the frequency (daily, weekly, etc.) and the time of day when the refresh should occur. Consider factors like user requirements, data source update intervals, and system availability.

4. Authentication and Credentials: Ensure that your data source credentials are securely stored and periodically updated. This includes using secure authentication methods and credentials that have the necessary permissions for data access.

5. Monitoring and Logging: Implement monitoring and logging mechanisms to track the status of data refreshes. This helps identify issues and bottlenecks, ensuring data refresh remains reliable.

6. Testing and Validation: Before deploying your scheduled refresh, perform thorough testing to validate that the process works as expected. This involves running refreshes in a controlled environment to detect and resolve potential issues.

Example of Scheduling Data Refresh:

Let's consider a real-world example to illustrate scheduling data refresh:

Example: A retail company uses Power BI to create sales reports that are shared with regional managers. To ensure timely insights, they schedule a daily data refresh for their reports.

Steps:

1. Data Connection: The company connects Power BI to their SQL Server database, which contains daily sales data.

2. Gateway Configuration: They set up a Data Gateway on a server that has access to the SQL Server database. The gateway is named and configured with a recovery key for data security.

3. Data Refresh Policies: The data refresh policy is configured to run daily at 2:00 AM. This timing ensures minimal disruption to the regional managers who access the reports.

4. Authentication and Credentials: The company uses secure SQL Server authentication and securely stores the database credentials within Power BI.

5. Monitoring and Logging: Power BI's built-in monitoring tools allow them to track the success of each refresh. Any failures or delays are immediately detected and addressed.

6. Testing and Validation: Before deploying the scheduled refresh to all regional managers, the IT department tests the process extensively to ensure that it performs reliably and error-free.

Conclusion:

Scheduling data refresh is pivotal to maintaining the accuracy and relevance of your Power Query reports and dashboards. By following best practices, ensuring reliable data connections, and running rigorous tests, organizations can automate data refresh processes and provide users with current and valuable insights for data-driven decision-making.

CHAPTER V
Advanced Power Query Topics

Part 13. Advanced M Language Techniques

13.1 Mastering the M Language

In this chapter, we delve deep into mastering the M language, a powerful tool for data transformation and manipulation within Power Query. The M language is at the core of Power Query, and understanding it thoroughly is essential for harnessing the full potential of this tool. This section provides a comprehensive guide to help you become proficient in M language techniques.

The Significance of Mastering the M Language:

Mastering the M language is crucial for several reasons:

1. Custom Data Transformations: M language allows you to create custom data transformations tailored to your specific needs. This empowers you to solve complex data challenges efficiently.

2. Optimized Data Processing: A deep understanding of M language enables you to write more efficient queries, resulting in faster data processing and reduced refresh times.

3. Complex Data Structures: You can work with complex data structures, such as lists, records, and tables, effectively by mastering M language constructs.

Key Concepts in Mastering the M Language:

- Syntax and Structure: Understanding the syntax and structure of the M language is the foundation. We'll cover the building blocks of M, including expressions, functions, and operators.

- Data Types: M language supports various data types, such as text, numbers, dates, and records. We'll explore how to work with these data types and perform type conversions.

- Transformations: Learn about the different types of transformations, including filtering, sorting, grouping, and aggregation. Master how to apply these transformations to your data effectively.

- Custom Functions: Create custom functions in M language, allowing you to encapsulate complex logic and reuse it across multiple queries.

- Advanced Techniques: Delve into advanced techniques like error handling, conditional logic, and handling null values within M language queries.

Illustrative Examples:

Let's consider an example to demonstrate the importance of mastering the M language:

Example: Suppose you're working with a dataset that contains sales data, and you need to create a calculated column that shows the year-to-date (YTD) total for each product. Mastering the M language would enable you to efficiently create a custom function in Power Query that calculates the YTD total based on the data's date column, product ID, and sales values. This custom function can then be applied to your dataset with ease.

Here is a simplified code snippet in M language for calculating YTD totals:

```M
let

    CalculateYTD = (table as table, dateColumn as text, productIDColumn as text, salesColumn as text) =>

    let

        // Group the table by product and calculate YTD sales

        grouped = Table.Group(table, {productIDColumn}, {

            {"YTD Total", each List.Sum([salesColumn]), type number}

        })

    in

        grouped

in

    CalculateYTD
```

This is just a glimpse of what can be accomplished when you master the M language. Through the extensive coverage of M language techniques in this chapter, you'll become proficient in creating custom transformations and solving complex data challenges.

Conclusion:

Mastering the M language is a pivotal skill for anyone working with Power Query for data transformation and shaping. It opens up a world of possibilities for custom data transformations, optimization, and handling complex data structures. This chapter will equip you with the knowledge and skills needed to leverage the full potential of the M language in your data projects.

In this section, we'll provide several examples to help you understand the M language and how to work with it effectively.

Example 1: Basic M Function

Let's start with a basic M function:

```M
let
    MultiplyByTwo = (x) => x * 2
in
    MultiplyByTwo
```

- `let`: This keyword is used to introduce a local variable named `MultiplyByTwo`.

- `(x)`: `x` is the parameter of the function.

- `=>`: It signifies the beginning of the function body.

- `x * 2`: This is the expression that defines what the function does. It multiplies the input value `x` by 2.

In this example, we define a simple function called `MultiplyByTwo`. It takes a single parameter `x` and returns the result of multiplying `x` by 2.

Example 2: Combining Text

Now, let's look at an example that combines text:

```M
let
    CombineText = (text1, text2) => text1 & ", " & text2
in
    CombineText
```

- `let`: We introduce the local variable `CombineText`.

- `(text1, text2)`: The function takes two text parameters, `text1` and `text2`.

- `=>`: It marks the start of the function body.

- `text1 & ", " & text2`: In this case, we concatenate the two text values with a comma and a space in between.

This example demonstrates a function named `CombineText` that takes two text inputs and returns them as a combined string separated by a comma and a space.

Example 3: Conditional Function

Let's explore a more advanced example involving conditionals:

```M
let
    AssignGrade = (score) =>
        if score >= 90 then "A"
        else if score >= 80 then "B"
        else if score >= 70 then "C"
        else "D"
in
    AssignGrade
```

- `let`: We introduce the function `AssignGrade`.

- `(score)`: The function parameter is `score`.

- `=>`: The function body starts here.

- if-else statements: Depending on the value of `score`, this function returns a letter grade ("A," "B," "C," or "D").

In this example, we define the `AssignGrade` function, which assigns a letter grade based on the provided `score`. It showcases how M functions can handle conditional logic.

These examples illustrate the syntax and usage of the M language. By mastering M, you can manipulate and transform data effectively in Power Query.

13.2 Custom Functions with Parameters

In this chapter, we explore the powerful world of custom functions with parameters within the M language. Custom functions provide the flexibility to encapsulate specific data transformation logic and make it reusable across different parts of your Power Query project. We will delve into the details of creating custom functions with parameters, making them versatile tools in your data transformation toolkit.

The Importance of Custom Functions with Parameters:

Custom functions with parameters offer the following advantages:

1. Reusability: You can define a function with parameters that allow you to apply the same logic to various data sources and scenarios, enhancing reusability.

2. Modularity: Custom functions promote modular code design. By breaking down complex transformations into smaller, parameterized functions, you can maintain and update your queries more efficiently.

3. Flexibility: Parameters make functions adaptable to different data structures and conditions, reducing the need for repetitive code.

Key Concepts in Custom Functions with Parameters:

- Defining Functions: We will cover the step-by-step process of defining custom functions with parameters. This includes specifying function names, input parameters, and the logic to apply to your data.

- Parameter Types: Understand different parameter types, including text, numbers, tables, and lists, and how to work with them in your functions.

- Optional and Default Parameters: Learn how to make certain parameters optional and set default values, allowing for greater flexibility when applying the function.

- Parameterized Transformations: Explore various data transformation scenarios using custom functions with parameters. We'll look at examples of filtering, aggregation, and data shaping, all tailored to specific needs.

Illustrative Examples:

Let's consider an example to illustrate the concept of custom functions with parameters:

Example: You have a dataset containing sales data, and you want to create a custom function that calculates the average sales for a specified time period, based on a date column and a sales value column. The function should take parameters for the date range and return the average sales within that range.

Here's a simplified custom function with parameters in M language:

```M
let
```

```
    CalculateAverageSales = (table as table, startDate as date, endDate as date, dateColumn as
text, salesColumn as text) =>

    let

        // Filter the table based on the date range

        filteredTable = Table.SelectRows(table, each [dateColumn] >= startDate and [dateColumn]
<= endDate),

        // Calculate the average sales

        averageSales = List.Average(filteredTable[salesColumn])

    in

        averageSales

in

    CalculateAverageSales
```

You can apply this custom function by specifying the date range, date column, and sales column. It will return the average sales for that period.

Conclusion:

Custom functions with parameters are a vital component of your data transformation workflow. They enable you to create reusable, versatile, and modular functions that adapt to various data scenarios. This chapter will equip you with the knowledge and practical skills to harness the full potential of custom functions with parameters in Power Query, making your data transformations more efficient and flexible.

In this section, we'll delve into creating custom M functions that take parameters and provide examples with explanations for each line of code.

Example 1: Custom Function for Simple Multiplication

Let's start with a custom function that multiplies two numbers:

```M
(Multiplier) => (x, y) => x * y * Multiplier
```

- `(Multiplier)`: This part declares the parameter `Multiplier`, which is a constant multiplier for the function.

- `=>`: It signifies the beginning of the inner function, which takes two parameters `x` and `y`.

- `x * y * Multiplier`: The function returns the product of `x`, `y`, and the constant `Multiplier`.

In this example, we define a custom function with a parameter `Multiplier`. The function takes two additional parameters, `x` and `y`, and multiplies them by `Multiplier`. You can use this function to apply a common factor to the multiplication of two numbers.

Example 2: Custom Function for Concatenating Text

Now, let's create a custom function for combining text:

```M
(Joiner) => (text1, text2) => text1 & Joiner & text2
```

- `(Joiner)`: Here, we declare the parameter `Joiner`, which is the character used to join the text.

- `=>`: It marks the beginning of the inner function that takes `text1` and `text2` as parameters.

- `text1 & Joiner & text2`: The function returns `text1`, followed by `Joiner`, and then `text2`.

In this example, we define a custom function that concatenates two text values with a character specified by the parameter `Joiner`. This allows flexibility in joining text with different delimiters.

Example 3: Custom Function for Conditional Grading

Let's explore a more complex example with conditional grading:

```M
(PassThreshold) => (score) =>
    if score >= PassThreshold then "Pass"
    else "Fail"
```

- `(PassThreshold)`: We declare a parameter `PassThreshold`, representing the minimum score for passing.

- `=>`: This marks the beginning of the inner function, which takes `score` as a parameter.

- if-else statement: The function checks if `score` is greater than or equal to `PassThreshold` and returns "Pass" or "Fail" accordingly.

In this example, we create a custom function that assesses whether a score passes based on a specified threshold (`PassThreshold`). By utilizing parameters, this function allows you to adapt the passing criterion as needed.

Custom functions with parameters in M language provide versatility and reusability in your data transformation and manipulation tasks within Power Query. They allow you to tailor functions to specific requirements by passing parameters as inputs.

13.3 Recursive Functions

In this chapter, we dive into the intriguing world of recursive functions within the M language. Recursive functions are a powerful tool for solving problems that involve repetitive or hierarchical data structures. They allow a function to call itself, making it especially useful for scenarios such as hierarchical data processing and iterative calculations.

The Significance of Recursive Functions:

Recursive functions offer unique advantages in data transformation:

1. Hierarchical Data Processing: Recursive functions are essential for handling hierarchical data structures, such as organizational charts, family trees, or bill of materials.

2. Iterative Calculations: They enable iterative calculations where each step relies on the results of the previous one, which is common in financial modeling and simulations.

3. Code Simplicity: Recursive functions simplify complex problems by breaking them down into smaller, repeatable steps.

Key Concepts in Recursive Functions:

- Defining Recursive Functions: We'll cover the fundamentals of creating recursive functions in M language, including establishing the base case and defining the recursive step.

- Base Case: Understand the importance of defining a base case in recursive functions. The base case specifies when the recursion should stop, preventing infinite loops.

- Recursive Step: Learn how to design the recursive step, which outlines the process of making the function call itself with modified input.

- Accumulators: Explore the use of accumulators in recursive functions to collect and combine results as the function traverses the data structure.

Illustrative Examples:

Let's consider a classic example of a recursive function: calculating the factorial of a number.

Example: Calculate the factorial of a positive integer using a recursive function.

```M
let
    Factorial = (n as number) =>
        if n <= 1 then
```

        1
    else
        n * Factorial(n - 1)
in
    Factorial
```

In this example, the base case checks if `n` is less than or equal to 1, in which case it returns 1. If `n` is greater than 1, the function calls itself with a modified input `n - 1`, effectively calculating the factorial of `n` by multiplying it with the factorial of `n - 1`. This is a classic example of recursion, and it's a simple yet illustrative case.

Conclusion:

Recursive functions are a valuable addition to your M language toolkit. They provide an elegant solution to problems involving repetitive or hierarchical data structures. This chapter will equip you with a solid understanding of how to define and apply recursive functions in Power Query, enabling you to tackle a wide range of data transformation challenges with efficiency and clarity.

Recursive functions are functions that call themselves, which can be useful for solving problems that involve repetitive or nested operations. Let's explore a few examples of recursive functions in M language and explain each line of code.

Example 1: Calculating Factorial Recursively

In this example, we'll create a recursive function to calculate the factorial of a number:

```M

Factorial = (n) =>

    if n <= 1 then 1

    else n * Factorial(n - 1)

```

- `Factorial = (n) =>`: This line defines a function named `Factorial` that takes one parameter `n`.

- `if n <= 1 then 1`: This is the base case of the recursion. If `n` is less than or equal to 1, the function returns 1. This is crucial to stop the recursion.

- `else n * Factorial(n - 1)`: In the recursive case, the function multiplies `n` by the result of calling `Factorial` with `n - 1`. This is the recursive step.

With this function, you can calculate the factorial of any non-negative integer `n`. For example, `Factorial(5)` will return `120`.

Example 2: Recursive Function for Fibonacci Sequence

Here's a recursive function to calculate the nth number in the Fibonacci sequence:

```M
Fibonacci = (n) =>

    if n <= 1 then n

    else Fibonacci(n - 1) + Fibonacci(n - 2)

```
```

- `Fibonacci = (n) =>`: This line defines the `Fibonacci` function that takes one parameter `n`.

- `if n <= 1 then n`: In the base case, if `n` is 0 or 1, the function returns `n`.

- `else Fibonacci(n - 1) + Fibonacci(n - 2)`: In the recursive case, the function returns the sum of two recursive calls to `Fibonacci` with `n - 1` and `n - 2`. This is the essence of the Fibonacci sequence.

This function allows you to find the nth Fibonacci number. For instance, `Fibonacci(7)` will yield `13`.

Example 3: Recursive Function for Generating a Range of Numbers

This example demonstrates a recursive function to generate a range of numbers from `start` to `end`:

```M
GenerateRange = (start, end) =>
    if start > end then []
    else start & GenerateRange(start + 1, end)
```

- `GenerateRange = (start, end) =>`: We define the `GenerateRange` function with two parameters, `start` and `end`.

- `if start > end then []`: If `start` exceeds `end`, the function returns an empty list, indicating the end of the range.

- `else start & GenerateRange(start + 1, end)`: In the recursive case, the function concatenates `start` with the result of a recursive call to `GenerateRange` with `start + 1` and the same `end`.

This function generates a list of numbers from `start` to `end`. For example, `GenerateRange(1, 5)` produces `[1, 2, 3, 4, 5]`.

Recursive functions in M language allow you to solve problems that involve repeating patterns or complex calculations by breaking them down into smaller, manageable steps. They often include a base case to terminate the recursion and a recursive step that makes the function call itself with modified parameters.

Part 14. Handling Data Errors and Anomalies

14.1 Identifying and Handling Data Errors

In this section, we will explore techniques for identifying and handling data errors in Power Query. Data errors can include missing values, inconsistent data types, outliers, or any issues that affect the data's quality and reliability. It is essential to detect and address these errors to ensure the accuracy of your analysis. Here, we will discuss several methods and provide practical examples.

Methods for Identifying Data Errors:

1. Missing Values Detection: Missing data can significantly impact your analysis. Power Query allows you to identify missing values and take specific actions, such as filling in missing values with defaults or removing rows with missing data.

```M
// Detect and Replace Missing Values with 0

Table.ReplaceValue(#"YourTable", 0, each if [ColumnName] = null then 0 else [ColumnName], Replacer.ReplaceValue, {"ColumnName"})
```

2. Data Type Inconsistencies: Ensuring consistent data types is crucial. You can identify and change data types using functions like `Table.TransformColumnTypes`.

```M
// Convert a Column to Date Type

Table.TransformColumnTypes(#"YourTable", {{"DateColumn", type date}})
```

```

3. Outliers Detection: Outliers can skew your analysis. You can use statistical methods like Z-scores to detect and handle outliers.

```M

// Detect and Replace Outliers with Median

let

    Source = YourTable,

    MedianValue = List.Median(Source[ColumnWithOutliers]),

    StDev = List.StandardDeviation(Source[ColumnWithOutliers]),

    ZScores = Table.AddColumn(Source, "Z-Score", each ([ColumnWithOutliers] - MedianValue) / StDev),

    FilteredTable = Table.SelectRows(ZScores, each [Z-Score] <= 3),

    ReplacedOutliers = Table.ReplaceValue(FilteredTable, MedianValue, each if [Z-Score] > 3 then MedianValue else [ColumnWithOutliers], Replacer.ReplaceValue, {"ColumnWithOutliers", "Z-Score"})

in

    ReplacedOutliers

```

Handling Data Errors:

1. Fill Missing Values: When you detect missing values, you can use functions like `Table.FillDown` to replace them with preceding values or defaults.
```

2. Remove Rows with Errors: To eliminate rows with data errors, use `Table.SelectRows` with appropriate criteria.

3. Standardize Data Types: You can use `Table.TransformColumnTypes` to ensure consistent data types.

4. Impute Outliers: When handling outliers, you can replace them with more representative values, like the median.

The key to dealing with data errors is to detect them early in your Power Query process and apply appropriate actions. By doing so, you can ensure your data is clean and reliable, setting the stage for accurate and insightful analysis. Always consider the specific needs of your data and analysis when deciding how to handle errors.

14.2 Detecting Anomalies and Outliers

In this section, we delve into the crucial process of detecting anomalies and outliers within your data using Power Query. Detecting these irregular data points is essential for maintaining data integrity and ensuring that your analysis is based on accurate and representative information.

Methods for Detecting Anomalies and Outliers:

1. Z-Score Calculation: One of the most common methods for detecting anomalies is calculating the Z-score for each data point in a column. The Z-score measures how many standard deviations a data point is from the mean. Any data point with an absolute Z-score above a certain threshold is considered an outlier.

```M
// Calculate Z-Score for a Column
```

let

    Source = YourTable,

    MeanValue = List.Average(Source[YourColumn]),

    StDev = List.StandardDeviation(Source[YourColumn]),

    ZScores = Table.AddColumn(Source, "Z-Score", each ([YourColumn] - MeanValue) / StDev)

in

    ZScores
```

2. Box Plots: Another visual method for identifying outliers is by creating box plots. Box plots provide a graphical representation of data distribution, highlighting any data points outside the "whiskers" as potential outliers.

```M
// Create a Box Plot
let

    Source = YourTable,

    BoxPlot = Table.BoxPlot(Source, {"YourColumn"})

in

    BoxPlot
```

3. IQR (Interquartile Range) Method: The IQR is the range between the first quartile (Q1) and the third quartile (Q3). Any data points outside this range are considered outliers.
```

```M
// Detect Outliers using IQR
let
    Source = YourTable,
    Q1 = List.FirstN(List.Sort(Source[YourColumn]),
Number.RoundDown(Table.RowCount(Source) * 0.25)),
    Q3 = List.LastN(List.Sort(Source[YourColumn]),
Number.RoundDown(Table.RowCount(Source) * 0.25)),
    IQR = Q3 - Q1,
    LowerBound = Q1 - 1.5 * IQR,
    UpperBound = Q3 + 1.5 * IQR,
    Outliers = Table.SelectRows(Source, each [YourColumn] < LowerBound or [YourColumn] > UpperBound)
in
    Outliers
```

Handling Detected Anomalies and Outliers:

Once you've detected anomalies and outliers, the next step is to decide how to handle them:

1. Remove Outliers: You can choose to remove data points identified as outliers if they are erroneous or don't fit the context of your analysis.

2. Transform or Impute: In some cases, you may want to transform or impute outliers rather than removing them. For instance, you could cap outliers at a certain threshold or replace them with a more representative value like the median.

3. Flag Outliers: You can also add a flag or a new column to your data to indicate which data points are outliers. This way, you retain the information while clearly identifying these values.

It's important to customize your approach based on the nature of your data and your analysis goals. This section equips you with the knowledge and tools needed to make informed decisions regarding anomalies and outliers in your datasets, ensuring the reliability and integrity of your analyses.

14.3 Implementing Data Validation

In this section, we explore the critical aspect of implementing data validation within Power Query. Data validation is the process of verifying the correctness and quality of your data to ensure that it meets specific criteria or business rules. By incorporating data validation into your Power Query workflows, you can improve data accuracy, consistency, and reliability.

Methods for Implementing Data Validation:

1. Data Type Validation: Ensuring that the data in a column adheres to the correct data type is a fundamental step. For example, you can validate that a column intended for dates only contains valid date values.

```M
// Data Type Validation for Date Column
let
    Source = YourTable,
    Validated = Table.TransformColumnTypes(Source, {{"DateColumn", type date}})
in
```

        Validated

```

2. Range and Boundary Validation: Checking if the data falls within specified ranges or boundaries. For instance, you can validate that values in a price column are within a reasonable price range.

```M
// Range Validation for Price Column
let
    Source = YourTable,
    Validated = Table.SelectRows(Source, each [Price] >= 0 and [Price] <= 1000)
in
    Validated
```

3. Duplicate Data Detection: Identifying and handling duplicate records is crucial for maintaining data quality. You can detect duplicate rows based on specific columns.

```M
// Duplicate Data Detection
let
    Source = YourTable,
    Validated = Table.Distinct(Source, {"Column1", "Column2"})
in
    Validated
```
```

4. Pattern Matching: You can implement validation based on specific patterns or formats. For example, validating email addresses or phone numbers to ensure they conform to expected patterns.

```M
// Pattern Matching for Email Addresses

let

    Source = YourTable,

    Validated = Table.SelectRows(Source, each Text.RegexMatch([Email], "^[a-zA-Z0-9._%+-]+@[a-zA-Z0-9.-]+\.[a-zA-Z]{2,4}$"))

in

    Validated
```

5. Custom Validation Rules: Define custom validation rules based on your specific business requirements. This can include complex rules that are unique to your organization.

```M
// Custom Data Validation Rule

let

    Source = YourTable,

    Validated = Table.SelectRows(Source, each [Column1] > [Column2] and [Column3] <> "Invalid")

in

    Validated
```

Handling Validation Errors:

When implementing data validation, it's essential to consider how to handle validation errors:

1. Reject Rows: You can choose to reject rows that do not meet the validation criteria. These rows can be removed from the dataset entirely.

2. Flag Validation Errors: Another approach is to add a new column or a flag indicating rows that contain validation errors. This way, you retain the information while making errors easily identifiable.

3. Impute or Transform Data: In some cases, you might prefer to correct or impute data to meet validation criteria rather than removing it.

4. Error Logging: Consider creating an error log to capture and analyze validation errors for auditing or reporting purposes.

Implementing data validation is a powerful way to ensure the quality and reliability of your data before using it in analytical or reporting tasks. This section equips you with the knowledge and techniques needed to integrate data validation seamlessly into your Power Query workflows, enhancing the overall data integrity and usefulness.

Part 15. Extending Power Query with Custom Connectors

15.1 Developing Custom Data Connectors

In this section, we will delve into the exciting world of developing custom data connectors for Power Query. Custom connectors allow you to expand Power Query's capabilities by integrating data sources that may not be natively supported. Whether it's connecting to an internal database, a proprietary web service, or a unique data format, custom connectors provide the flexibility to access a wide range of data.

Why Develop Custom Data Connectors:

1. Accessing Specialized Data Sources: Custom connectors enable you to connect to specialized data sources, such as in-house databases, legacy systems, or proprietary APIs that are not covered by standard connectors.

2. Streamlining Data Retrieval: You can develop connectors to retrieve data efficiently by implementing custom logic tailored to your data source.

3. Automation and Consistency: Custom connectors can automate data retrieval processes, ensuring consistent and up-to-date data for your Power Query transformations.

Key Steps in Developing Custom Data Connectors:

1. Setting up the Development Environment: You'll need tools like Power Query SDK (Software Development Kit) and Visual Studio to develop custom connectors. Once set up, you can start the development process.

2. Creating Connector Functions: Develop custom functions that define how to connect to your data source, retrieve data, and handle authentication.

```M
// Example Custom Connector Function

(dataSourcePath) =>

let

    // Define connection logic here

    source = SomeCustomFunction(dataSourcePath)

in

    source
```

3. Defining Data Source Options: Specify the required options and parameters for your custom connector. This could include connection strings, API keys, and other settings.

```M
// Custom Data Source Options

[

    Option1 = "Value1",

    Option2 = "Value2"

]
```

4. Testing and Debugging: Thoroughly test your custom connector to ensure it functions correctly. Use tools like the Power Query SDK to troubleshoot and debug any issues.

5. Documentation: Document your custom connector, including how to use it, the expected parameters, and any specific requirements.

Practical Example:

Let's say you want to develop a custom connector to retrieve data from your organization's proprietary RESTful API. You'd define the connection details, the authentication method (such as an API key or OAuth token), and the data retrieval process.

Once your custom connector is ready, users can access it through Power Query, just like built-in connectors. They can provide the necessary parameters and retrieve data seamlessly.

Developing custom data connectors is an advanced but incredibly valuable skill. It opens up a world of possibilities for integrating diverse data sources into your Power Query workflows. This section equips you with the knowledge and guidance to get started, enabling you to create connectors tailored to your unique data needs.

15.2 Using Third-Party Connectors

In this section, we will explore the integration of third-party connectors into Power Query, broadening your ability to access a wide range of data sources. Third-party connectors are pre-built, often specialized, connectors developed by external vendors or the community. These connectors offer a convenient way to access unique data sources without having to create custom connectors from scratch.

Why Use Third-Party Connectors:

1. Expand Data Source Options: Third-party connectors enhance your Power Query capabilities by providing access to data sources that aren't covered by standard connectors. This can include cloud services, databases, APIs, and more.

2. Time and Resource Efficiency: By using third-party connectors, you save time and resources that would otherwise be spent on developing custom connectors. They are ready-made for immediate use.

3. Community-Driven: Many third-party connectors are community-driven and frequently updated, ensuring ongoing support and improved compatibility with evolving data sources.

How to Use Third-Party Connectors:

1. Search and Install: In Power Query, you can browse a gallery of third-party connectors, often available through the Power Query Online Services. You can search for connectors that suit your needs and install them directly.

2. Configuration: Configure the third-party connector by providing any required parameters, such as authentication keys, connection details, or API tokens.

3. Data Retrieval: After installation and configuration, you can use the third-party connector just like built-in connectors. Select the connector, enter the necessary parameters, and retrieve the data.

Practical Example:

Imagine you need to access data from a specific cloud storage platform that doesn't have a native Power Query connector. Instead of creating a custom connector, you can search for a third-party connector that connects to this cloud service.

Once you've found the appropriate third-party connector, install it, provide the required credentials or configuration details, and retrieve the data seamlessly. This simplifies the process and avoids the need for custom development.

This section will guide you through the steps of searching for, installing, configuring, and using third-party connectors effectively. You'll learn how to harness the power of these connectors to access diverse data sources with ease, saving time and expanding your data integration capabilities.

15.3 Enhancing Data Source Connectivity

This section delves into the strategies and techniques for enhancing your data source connectivity within Power Query. While developing custom data connectors and utilizing third-party connectors significantly broaden your options, you can take further steps to optimize data retrieval, ensure data quality, and improve the overall data source connectivity.

Improving Data Source Connectivity:

1. Data Source Performance Optimization: Fine-tuning your queries and optimizing data source interactions is crucial for efficient data retrieval. This can involve refining query folding, applying filters and transformations closer to the source, and reducing unnecessary data transfer.

2. Caching Data: Power Query allows you to cache data at various stages of your data transformation process. By caching intermediate data, you can reduce the need to re-fetch data from the source, leading to faster query performance.

3. Incremental Data Loading: When dealing with large datasets, implementing incremental data loading can significantly speed up data refresh processes. This approach involves only retrieving new or changed data from the source instead of fetching the entire dataset.

4. Data Source Security: Ensuring the security of your data source connections is paramount. You can enhance data source connectivity by implementing encryption, securing credentials, and complying with data privacy regulations.

Practical Examples:

1. Optimizing SQL Queries: Suppose you're connecting to a relational database using Power Query. To enhance data source connectivity, you can optimize SQL queries to minimize the amount of data transferred. This could involve using indexed columns, writing efficient queries, and filtering data closer to the source.

2. Caching for Repeated Queries: If you frequently access the same data, enabling data caching can be highly beneficial. By storing intermediate results, you save time and resources when re-executing similar queries.

3. Incremental Data Loading for Sales Data: In scenarios where you're dealing with daily sales data, implementing incremental data loading can dramatically reduce the data refresh time. You can set up your queries to only retrieve the sales transactions since the last refresh, eliminating the need to reload historical data.

4. Securing API Connections: When connecting to external APIs, ensuring data source security is crucial. Implementing API keys, OAuth authentication, and encryption can enhance connectivity while keeping your data secure.

This section will provide you with comprehensive insights into these strategies, equipping you with the knowledge to optimize your data source connectivity. You'll learn how to fine-tune queries, apply caching effectively, set up incremental data loading, and prioritize data source security, ensuring efficient and secure data retrieval for your Power Query projects.

CHAPTER VI
Integrating Power Query with Other Tools

Part 16. Power Query and Power Pivot Integration

16.1 Creating Data Models in Power Pivot

In this section, we will explore the seamless integration of Power Query with Power Pivot, a powerful feature in Excel and Power BI for creating data models. By creating data models in Power Pivot, you can transform and shape your data using Power Query and then build relationships, measures, and advanced data analysis capabilities. Let's dive into the details:

Overview:

Power Pivot allows you to create data models that can handle large volumes of data efficiently. It's an essential tool when you need to analyze and visualize data using PivotTables, PivotCharts, and more advanced features.

Steps to Create Data Models in Power Pivot:

1. Data Load: Start by using Power Query to load and transform your data. This can involve merging tables, cleaning data, and creating calculated columns, as discussed in earlier chapters.

2. Data Model Creation: Once your data is ready, you can load it into Power Pivot. To do this, enable the Power Pivot add-in if you haven't already. Then, select the tables you want to include in your data model.

3. Defining Relationships: One of the key benefits of Power Pivot is the ability to create relationships between tables. These relationships help you combine data from different tables for more comprehensive analysis.

4. Measures and Calculated Columns: In Power Pivot, you can create measures and calculated columns using Data Analysis Expressions (DAX). Measures are calculations that provide aggregated results, while calculated columns allow you to add custom columns to your tables.

5. Advanced Data Analysis: Power Pivot offers advanced features like time-intelligence functions, What-If analysis, and pattern recognition through DAX. These functionalities can help you gain deeper insights from your data.

Practical Example:

Imagine you have sales data from multiple regions and want to analyze the overall performance of your products. You can use Power Query to clean and merge sales data from various sources, such as different Excel files and a database. Once the data is ready, you load it into Power Pivot, establish relationships between tables (e.g., Sales, Products, Regions), and create measures (e.g., Total Sales, Average Price).

By doing so, you can create PivotTables that provide instant insights into your sales data, showing performance across regions, products, and time periods. With DAX, you can build custom calculations like Year-over-Year growth, market share, and sales forecasting.

By following these steps and leveraging Power Pivot's capabilities, you can create sophisticated data models in Excel and Power BI that support advanced data analysis and visualization, providing valuable insights to drive informed decision-making. This integration between Power Query and Power Pivot is a powerful approach to transforming and analyzing data.

16.2 Building Relationships and Measures

In this section, we will delve into the critical aspect of building relationships and creating measures within Power Pivot. These functionalities are central to unleashing the full potential of your data models and enabling advanced data analysis capabilities in Excel and Power BI.

Understanding Relationships:

In Power Pivot, relationships are the connections between different tables within your data model. Building relationships is essential because they allow you to combine data from multiple tables effectively. You can create relationships based on common fields, such as primary and foreign keys.

Steps to Build Relationships:

1. Identify Tables: First, you need to identify the tables in your data model that contain related information. For example, if you have tables for sales, products, and customers, you may want to create relationships between them.

2. Common Fields: Determine the common fields or columns in these tables that will serve as the basis for your relationships. Typically, these are fields that share related information, like a product ID or a customer ID.

3. Establish Relationships: Create relationships by defining how these common fields are related. You specify whether it's a one-to-one, one-to-many, or many-to-many relationship. Additionally, you indicate which table plays the role of the primary table and which is the related table.

4. Enforce Referential Integrity: You have the option to enforce referential integrity, which ensures that data remains consistent across related tables. This means that if a record in the primary table is deleted or modified, corresponding records in the related table are also updated or deleted, maintaining data integrity.

Creating Measures:

Measures are calculations that provide aggregated results for your data. They allow you to perform computations on your data, such as summing sales, calculating averages, or finding minimum and maximum values. Measures are expressed using Data Analysis Expressions (DAX), a powerful formula language.

Steps to Create Measures:

1. Understand the Analysis Needs: Begin by understanding the analytical requirements of your data model. What specific calculations or aggregations are needed? For example, you might need measures like Total Sales, Average Price, or Year-over-Year Growth.

2. Write DAX Formulas: Using DAX, write formulas that define your measures. DAX includes functions and operators for a wide range of calculations. For instance, you can use the SUM function to calculate the total sales.

3. Test and Validate Measures: After creating your measures, test and validate them to ensure they provide the expected results. You can use PivotTables and PivotCharts to visualize the impact of your measures on your data.

Practical Example:

Imagine you have a data model containing tables for Sales, Products, and Customers. To analyze your data effectively, you create relationships between these tables based on common fields, such as Product ID and Customer ID. This allows you to connect sales with specific products and customers.

Next, you create measures using DAX, such as Total Sales, Average Price, and Year-over-Year Growth in Sales. These measures enable you to gain valuable insights into your data, such as the overall revenue, product performance, and sales trends over time.

By building relationships and measures, you transform your data model into a powerful analytical tool that can answer complex business questions and provide actionable insights. The integration of Power Query with Power Pivot empowers you to perform advanced data analysis within Excel and Power BI, making informed decisions based on your data.

16.3 Advanced Data Analysis in Excel and Power BI

In this section, we will explore the advanced data analysis capabilities that become accessible when you harness the combined power of Power Query and Power Pivot in both Excel and Power BI. Integrating these tools opens the door to conducting sophisticated data analysis, enabling you to derive meaningful insights and make data-driven decisions.

Leveraging Advanced Analysis Techniques:

1. Multi-Dimensional Analysis: With Power Pivot, you can perform multi-dimensional analysis by creating PivotTables and PivotCharts that provide a more comprehensive view of your data. This allows you to analyze data from multiple perspectives, drilling down into details or rolling up to see the big picture.

2. Time Intelligence Functions: Both Excel and Power BI offer time intelligence functions that enable you to analyze data across different time periods. You can calculate year-to-date, quarter-to-date, or month-to-month comparisons, making it easy to identify trends and patterns.

3. Advanced DAX Formulas: Data Analysis Expressions (DAX) allows you to write complex calculations and formulas to gain deeper insights. You can use DAX functions like SUMX, AVERAGEX, and CALCULATE to perform calculations involving multiple tables and conditions.

Data Modeling for Advanced Analysis:

1. Hierarchies: Power Pivot supports the creation of hierarchies, allowing you to structure data in a way that makes sense for your analysis. Hierarchies are beneficial for drilling down or rolling up data and facilitate interactive reports.

2. KPIs (Key Performance Indicators): Key performance indicators provide a straightforward way to evaluate performance against predefined targets or goals. You can create KPIs to visually represent the status of your data.

Visualization and Reporting:

1. Interactive Dashboards: In Power BI, you can design interactive dashboards that display key metrics and insights in real time. Users can explore data, filter information, and gain a dynamic understanding of your business performance.

2. Custom Visuals: Both Excel and Power BI allow you to incorporate custom visuals to represent data uniquely. You can import custom visualizations or even develop your own if needed.

Real-World Example:

Suppose you work in sales and have integrated Power Query and Power Pivot with your sales data in Excel and Power BI. You aim to perform advanced data analysis. With these tools:

- You can create PivotTables that break down sales data by region, product category, and time period simultaneously.

- Using time intelligence functions, you can compare sales performance year-over-year, identify seasonal trends, and track quarterly growth.

- Advanced DAX formulas enable you to calculate complex metrics, such as customer lifetime value, cohort analysis, and conversion rates.

- By defining hierarchies, you can navigate sales data at various levels, from yearly totals to daily transactions.

- You set up KPIs to monitor sales goals and visually highlight whether they are met.

- Interactive dashboards in Power BI provide a real-time snapshot of sales performance, and custom visuals help visualize data in innovative ways.

The integration of Power Query and Power Pivot with advanced data analysis techniques empowers Excel and Power BI users to conduct in-depth analysis, generate valuable insights, and share these insights effectively through interactive reports and dashboards. This capability is invaluable for businesses seeking to make informed decisions and gain a competitive edge in today's data-driven world.

Part 17. Power Query in Data Visualization Tools

17.1 Exporting Data to Tableau

Power Query is a powerful tool that allows you to transform and shape your data, making it suitable for various data visualization tools, including Tableau. In this section, we'll explore how to export data from Power Query to Tableau and harness the capabilities of both tools for effective data visualization and analysis.

Exporting Data to Tableau:

1. Data Preparation: The journey begins in Power Query, where you clean, reshape, and transform your data. This step is crucial to ensure that your data is in the desired format for analysis in Tableau. Power Query provides a user-friendly interface for performing these tasks.

2. Loading Data: Once your data is prepared, you can load it into Tableau. Tableau provides a straightforward method to connect to your data source, and you can choose the data connection type that suits your needs.

3. Maintaining Data Consistency: The advantage of using Power Query is that any changes made to your data source are automatically reflected in Tableau. You maintain data consistency by updating your Power Query queries whenever your data source changes. This ensures that your Tableau visualizations are always based on the most up-to-date data.

4. Tableau Visualizations: With your data now in Tableau, you can create various visualizations to gain insights. Tableau offers a wide range of chart types, including bar charts, scatter plots, heat maps, and more. You can drag and drop dimensions and measures to design interactive dashboards and reports.

Example Scenario:

Suppose you're an analyst in a retail company, and you've used Power Query to clean and shape your sales data, including information about products, sales channels, and customer demographics. Here's how you can export the data to Tableau:

1. In Power Query, you apply transformations to your sales data, such as merging tables, creating calculated columns, and removing duplicates.

2. You load the transformed data into Tableau, establishing a connection between Power Query and Tableau.

3. You create Tableau visualizations, such as a bar chart showing product sales by category, a scatter plot displaying the relationship between customer age and average purchase amount, and a heat map illustrating sales performance by region.

4. The beauty of this integration is that any changes you make to your sales data source in Power Query, like adding new sales records or updating product information, will automatically be reflected in Tableau. This ensures that your Tableau visualizations are always based on the latest data.

Exporting data from Power Query to Tableau streamlines your data preparation process and empowers you to create impactful data visualizations. It enhances your ability to uncover insights, make data-driven decisions, and share compelling stories with your organization.

17.2 Integrating Power Query with QlikView

QlikView is a powerful data visualization and business intelligence (BI) tool that empowers users to explore and analyze data interactively. Integrating Power Query with QlikView can enhance your data preparation capabilities and provide a more efficient way to work with your data. In this section, we will delve into how you can seamlessly integrate Power Query with QlikView.

Integrating Power Query with QlikView:

1. Data Preparation with Power Query: The journey starts in Power Query, a versatile ETL (Extract, Transform, Load) tool. Here, you can clean, transform, and shape your data as needed. Power Query offers a user-friendly interface and a wide range of data transformation capabilities.

2. Loading Data into QlikView: After you have prepared your data in Power Query, you can seamlessly load it into QlikView. QlikView provides multiple data connectivity options, and you can connect to various data sources, including files, databases, and web services.

3. Power Query Updates: One of the advantages of using Power Query is its ability to update your data source. Any changes made in Power Query, such as refreshing data or applying new transformations, are instantly reflected in QlikView. This ensures that your QlikView dashboards and reports are based on the most current data.

4. QlikView Data Modeling: With your data now in QlikView, you can create a data model using QlikView's associative data structure. This model enables you to establish relationships between data tables, making it easier to explore data and uncover insights.

Example Scenario:

Imagine you're an analyst in a healthcare organization, and you've utilized Power Query to clean and transform patient data, hospital records, and medical procedures. Here's how you can integrate Power Query with QlikView:

1. In Power Query, you perform data transformations like merging patient and hospital data, calculating the cost of medical procedures, and removing inconsistencies.

2. You load the transformed data into QlikView, creating a data model that connects different data tables. This model allows you to explore the relationships between patients, hospitals, and medical procedures.

3. With your QlikView model in place, you can create interactive dashboards and reports. For instance, you can visualize patient demographics, analyze hospital performance, and monitor the cost-effectiveness of medical procedures.

4. Any changes made in Power Query, such as adding new patient records or updating medical procedure information, are instantly reflected in QlikView, ensuring that your data analysis is always based on the latest data.

Integrating Power Query with QlikView enhances your data preparation and analysis capabilities. It enables you to explore data relationships, uncover insights, and create interactive data visualizations. This seamless integration streamlines your workflow, empowering you to make data-driven decisions and share valuable insights with your organization.

17.3 Using Power Query with other BI Tools

While we have explored integrating Power Query with specific data visualization tools like Tableau and QlikView, Power Query's versatility extends to other Business Intelligence (BI) tools as well. In this section, we will discuss how you can leverage Power Query in conjunction with various BI tools to enhance your data preparation and analysis processes.

Using Power Query with other BI Tools:

1. Data Source Connectivity: Power Query offers a wide range of connectors to access data from diverse sources such as databases, cloud services, web APIs, and more. When working with other BI tools, you can use Power Query to connect to these sources and retrieve data in a structured format.

2. Data Transformation and Cleaning: Power Query's strength lies in its ability to clean, transform, and shape data. Regardless of the BI tool you're using, you can use Power Query as a dedicated ETL tool to ensure your data is ready for analysis. This includes activities like filtering, merging, pivoting, and handling data errors.

3. Data Enrichment: Beyond basic transformations, Power Query allows you to enrich your data. You can merge data from multiple sources, add calculated columns, and apply custom transformations. This enriched data provides valuable context for your analysis.

4. Data Model Integration: When working with BI tools, a well-structured data model is essential. Power Query helps in creating this model by shaping data according to your needs. You can establish relationships between tables, create hierarchies, and organize your data for better insights.

Example Scenario:

Suppose you're a data analyst in a retail company, and your goal is to use data for business intelligence and reporting. You have data from various sources, including sales transactions, inventory, and customer information. Here's how you can use Power Query with various BI tools:

1. Data Connection: Power Query allows you to connect to sales databases, inventory systems, and customer databases, extracting data from each source.

2. Data Transformation: You utilize Power Query to clean and reshape the data. This involves filtering out incomplete sales records, merging customer data with sales transactions, and transforming inventory data into a usable format.

3. Data Enrichment: You add calculated columns to calculate sales revenue, customer lifetime value, and inventory turnover. Power Query enables you to merge external data sources, such as market trends and economic indicators, to provide a broader context for your analysis.

4. Data Modeling: With the transformed and enriched data, you create a data model using Power Query, establishing relationships between sales, inventory, and customer tables.

Now, when you use other BI tools like Microsoft Power BI, Tableau, or QlikView, you can seamlessly connect to this Power Query-prepared data. Your BI tool benefits from the clean and structured data, enabling you to create insightful dashboards and reports for decision-makers in your organization.

In summary, using Power Query with various BI tools is a versatile approach to data analysis. It provides a consistent and powerful data preparation foundation, ensuring that your data is ready for robust analysis and visualization, regardless of the BI tool you choose to work with.

Part 18. Automation and Scripting with Power Query

18.1 Automating Data Transformation Workflows

In this section, we will explore the powerful capabilities of Power Query in automating data transformation workflows. Power Query, which is known for its intuitive and interactive data preparation features, can also be harnessed to create automated processes that save you time, reduce manual errors, and ensure consistent data transformations.

Automating Data Transformation Workflows:

1. Query Parameters: Power Query allows you to set query parameters. These parameters serve as placeholders for values that can change over time, such as file paths or date ranges. By utilizing query parameters, you can create dynamic and reusable queries.

   Example: Consider a scenario where you receive monthly sales data files. With query parameters, you can set up a template query that dynamically adapts to the current month's data, ensuring a seamless update process.

2. Custom Functions: You can create custom functions in Power Query to encapsulate complex transformation logic. These functions can be reused across multiple queries, streamlining the transformation process.

   Example: Let's say you have various data sources that require specific cleaning operations. By designing custom functions for each type of data source, you can apply consistent transformations effortlessly.

3. Batch Processing: Power Query supports batch processing, enabling you to automate the transformation of multiple files in a folder. You can create queries that loop through files and apply the same transformations to each of them.

   Example: Imagine you have a directory of daily log files. With batch processing, you can automate the extraction, cleaning, and consolidation of data from all these log files into a single dataset.

4. Advanced Queries: Utilizing advanced M code, you can build robust data transformation workflows. This includes creating conditional transformations, handling exceptions, and applying specialized rules to your data.

   Example: Suppose you receive data from different vendors, each with unique data structures. With advanced queries, you can automatically detect the data structure for each vendor and apply the corresponding transformation logic.

Automation in Action:

Let's walk through an example of automating data transformation workflows using Power Query:

Scenario: You work for a retail company that receives sales data daily from multiple stores. Your goal is to automate the process of transforming and loading this data into your database for analysis.

Automation Steps:

1. Query Parameters: You set up query parameters to specify the source folder where the daily sales data files are stored. The parameter allows you to change the folder path as needed.

2. Custom Functions: You create a custom function that extracts data from each sales file, cleans it, and merges it into a master dataset. This function can be applied to all files in the source folder.

3. Batch Processing: You design a batch process query that iterates through the files in the specified folder. For each file, the custom function is called, resulting in automated data transformation.

4. Data Loading: After the data is transformed, you use Power Query to load it into your database, ensuring that the data is available for analysis.

By automating this process, you eliminate the need for manual intervention, save time, and ensure that your data is consistently transformed and ready for analysis. This is just one example of how Power Query's automation capabilities can be applied to streamline your data transformation workflows.

18.2 Scripting with Power Query

In this section, we delve into the world of scripting with Power Query. Scripting provides an advanced and flexible way to manipulate and transform your data using the M language. While Power Query's graphical interface is powerful, scripting allows you to perform intricate operations and create customized data transformation processes.

Scripting with Power Query:

1. Custom M Code: Power Query enables you to write custom M code within your queries. This code can be used to define complex data transformation steps that may not be achievable through the graphical interface alone.

   Example: You have a dataset with multiple date columns in different formats. By scripting custom M code, you can harmonize the date formats across the dataset, ensuring consistency.

2. Parameterized Scripts: You can create parameterized scripts, allowing you to reuse and adapt code for various scenarios. By defining parameters, your scripts become dynamic and adaptable, making it easy to apply the same logic to different datasets.

   Example: You want to standardize currency conversions for data from various countries. Using parameterized scripts, you can create a single script that accepts the currency exchange rate as a parameter, making it suitable for multiple currencies.

3. Conditional Logic: Scripting with Power Query enables you to incorporate conditional logic into your data transformation. This means you can create rules that respond to specific conditions within your data, automating the decision-making process.

   Example: Your sales data includes a "Region" column, and you want to categorize sales as high, medium, or low based on the region's performance. Scripting allows you to apply conditional logic to assign these categories dynamically.

4. Advanced Data Processing: Scripting provides a powerful platform for advanced data processing. You can implement recursive functions, sophisticated statistical calculations, and data cleansing operations that go beyond the standard capabilities of the graphical interface.

Example: You have a dataset with time series data, and you want to calculate moving averages for various time windows. Scripting allows you to create custom functions for calculating these moving averages.

Scripting in Action:

Let's illustrate the concept of scripting with Power Query through a practical example:

Scenario: You are working with a dataset that contains unstructured text data, and you want to extract specific information from it. The text data follows a consistent pattern, but it requires a custom extraction process.

Scripting Steps:

1. Custom M Code: You create a script with custom M code that defines the extraction logic. This code identifies patterns and extracts relevant data from the unstructured text.

2. Parameterized Script: To make your script adaptable, you parameterize it to accept user-defined keywords. Users can specify the keywords they want to extract from the text.

3. Conditional Logic: You incorporate conditional logic within the script to handle different scenarios. For instance, if a specific keyword is not found in the text, the script gracefully handles this situation.

4. Advanced Processing: To enhance the script's capabilities, you use recursive functions to extract data from nested structures within the text, providing a comprehensive extraction solution.

By scripting with Power Query, you have created a dynamic, adaptable, and powerful data transformation process. This example demonstrates how scripting allows you to tailor your data transformation to the unique requirements of your dataset, offering a level of precision and control that is invaluable in complex data scenarios.

18.3 Scheduling Data Refresh in a Production Environment

In this section, we explore the critical aspect of scheduling data refresh in a production environment when using Power Query. Ensuring that your data is up-to-date and accurate is fundamental to making informed decisions and maintaining the integrity of your data-driven processes.

Scheduling Data Refresh:

1. Data Source Considerations: Before implementing a data refresh schedule, it's essential to understand the nature of your data sources. Different data sources may require distinct refresh frequencies. For example, financial data may need daily updates, while customer demographics can be refreshed weekly.

   Example: Imagine you're managing a retail business with sales data coming from various store locations. Daily sales data is vital for monitoring daily performance, but inventory data may only need a weekly update.

2. Automation Tools: Power Query offers integration with various automation tools and services to facilitate scheduled data refresh. Understanding and selecting the right automation tool or service is crucial to ensure timely and reliable refreshes.

Example: You can use Azure Logic Apps to trigger Power Query data refresh at specific times or in response to specific events, such as the closure of daily sales.

3. Error Handling and Notifications: Implementing an effective error handling and notification system is essential for a production environment. In the event of a data refresh failure, you need a mechanism to detect issues and notify the relevant stakeholders promptly.

Example: If a scheduled refresh fails due to a data source connection issue, you can set up alerts and notifications to inform the data team or IT support for rapid resolution.

4. Refresh Dependencies: Complex datasets may have dependencies, where the refresh of one query is reliant on the successful refresh of another. Managing these dependencies is critical to maintaining data consistency.

Example: In a scenario where you have a master data query used by multiple other queries, you need to ensure that the master data query is refreshed before the dependent queries.

Scheduling Data Refresh in Action:

Let's illustrate the concept of scheduling data refresh in a production environment through a practical example:

Scenario: You work for an e-commerce company, and your Power Query data model combines sales data from multiple channels, customer data, and inventory data. The company operates 24/7, so data needs to be refreshed at various frequencies.

Data Refresh Strategy:

1. Sales Data: Sales data from online and offline stores is critical and must be updated daily to track real-time sales performance.

2. Customer Data: Customer demographics change less frequently, so a weekly refresh is sufficient.

3. Inventory Data: Inventory levels are updated monthly, so a monthly refresh schedule is appropriate.

Automation Tool: You decide to use Azure Data Factory for scheduling data refresh. It provides flexibility and integrates well with Power Query.

Error Handling: You set up email alerts and notifications for the data team and IT support. In case of refresh failures, relevant personnel are informed immediately.

Dependency Management: You ensure that sales data is refreshed first, followed by customer data and then inventory data. This sequence ensures that sales reports are always based on the latest data.

Scheduling data refresh in a production environment is a critical aspect of ensuring data accuracy and availability. The example above demonstrates how a data refresh strategy can be tailored to the unique needs of your organization, ensuring that your data-driven processes remain reliable and up-to-date.

CHAPTER VII
Power Query for Specialized Use Cases

Part 19. Power Query in Financial Analysis

19.1 Financial Data Extraction and Transformation

Financial analysis is a critical component of decision-making in the business world. Accessing, transforming, and analyzing financial data efficiently is paramount for making informed choices and assessing the health of a company. In this chapter, we'll explore how Power Query can revolutionize financial data extraction and transformation, helping you unlock valuable insights.

The Power of Power Query in Finance:

Financial data comes in various formats, from spreadsheets to databases, and extracting and consolidating this information can be a time-consuming process. Power Query streamlines this by providing powerful data transformation capabilities. Here's how it can benefit financial professionals:

- Data Extraction: Power Query allows you to connect to a multitude of data sources, including accounting software, market data providers, and more. We'll walk you through the process of extracting financial data from these sources.

- Data Transformation: Financial data can be messy, with inconsistent formatting and structures. Power Query's transformation capabilities enable you to clean, reshape, and structure your data for analysis. We'll delve into techniques for handling common financial data challenges.

- Data Enrichment: Sometimes, financial data needs enrichment with additional information, such as market indices, currency exchange rates, or economic indicators. Power Query enables you to combine data from various sources and enhance your financial datasets.

Practical Examples:

To illustrate these concepts, we'll work through real-world scenarios. You'll learn how to:

1. Retrieve Historical Stock Prices: We'll show you how to use Power Query to fetch historical stock prices from an online source, clean the data, and create informative visualizations for stock performance analysis.

2. Consolidate Financial Statements: Financial statements are a staple in financial analysis. You'll discover how to automate the extraction and consolidation of income statements, balance sheets, and cash flow statements from multiple subsidiaries or divisions.

3. Currency Conversion and Exchange Rates: For businesses operating internationally, managing multiple currencies is crucial. We'll guide you on how to use Power Query to perform currency conversion and stay updated with the latest exchange rates.

Empower Your Financial Analysis:

By the end of this chapter, you'll be equipped with the knowledge and skills to revolutionize your financial analysis workflows. Power Query will become your trusted ally in extracting, transforming, and enriching financial data, ensuring that you make data-driven financial decisions with confidence. Get ready to unlock the full potential of Power Query in the world of finance.

19.2 Building Financial Models

Financial modeling is the backbone of sound financial decision-making. It involves creating a representation of a financial system using various mathematical and logical tools. In this chapter, we will explore how Power Query can be a valuable asset in the process of building robust financial models for diverse financial scenarios.

The Power of Financial Modeling with Power Query:

Financial models provide a dynamic framework for assessing the financial performance and future prospects of a business. Power Query can significantly enhance the model-building process by streamlining data acquisition, transformation, and analysis. Here's how Power Query can empower financial modeling:

- Data Integration: Financial models often require data from different sources such as income statements, balance sheets, and operational data. Power Query enables you to effortlessly integrate these disparate datasets into a single cohesive source.

- Data Cleaning and Transformation: Data quality is paramount in financial modeling. Power Query's data cleaning and transformation features ensure that your financial data is accurate and consistent. We'll explore techniques for handling missing values, outliers, and irregularities.

- Scenario Analysis: Financial models often involve scenario analysis, where different assumptions are tested to assess their impact on financial outcomes. Power Query can expedite the process of preparing data for various scenarios and help in making informed decisions.

Practical Examples:

To illustrate the power of Power Query in building financial models, we will walk you through practical examples:

1. Creating a Cash Flow Forecast Model: We will demonstrate how to use Power Query to extract historical financial data, clean and transform it, and create a dynamic cash flow forecast model. This model can be used to assess the financial health of a company and make cash flow projections.

2. Monte Carlo Simulation: Monte Carlo simulations are frequently used in financial modeling to assess risk and uncertainty. We will show you how Power Query can prepare the data required for Monte Carlo simulations, enabling you to evaluate various financial scenarios.

3. Sensitivity Analysis: Sensitivity analysis involves changing key variables in a financial model to assess their impact. Power Query will assist in efficiently preparing datasets for sensitivity analysis, saving time and effort.

Elevate Your Financial Modeling Skills:

By the end of this chapter, you will have a deep understanding of how Power Query can streamline the process of building financial models. You will be able to harness its capabilities to create robust and flexible financial models that are essential for strategic decision-making in the world of finance. Prepare to take your financial modeling skills to the next level with the help of Power Query.

19.3 Risk Analysis and Scenario Planning

Risk analysis and scenario planning are fundamental aspects of financial decision-making, enabling organizations to anticipate and prepare for potential challenges and opportunities. In this chapter, we will delve into how Power Query can be a pivotal tool in conducting risk analysis and developing scenario planning models.

Leveraging Power Query for Risk Analysis:

Risk analysis involves assessing the potential impact of various risks on financial outcomes. Power Query can streamline the process by enabling financial professionals to acquire, transform, and analyze data efficiently. Here's how Power Query can be harnessed for risk analysis:

- Data Gathering: Power Query can help you consolidate data from different sources, such as historical financial records, market data, and industry trends, into a unified dataset for analysis.

- Data Enrichment: In risk analysis, it's essential to enhance raw data with additional information to make informed decisions. Power Query allows you to enrich data by connecting to online data sources, external databases, or APIs.

- Risk Modeling: We will explore how to use Power Query to prepare data for various risk modeling techniques, including Value at Risk (VaR), stress testing, and sensitivity analysis.

Scenario Planning with Power Query:

Scenario planning is a strategic approach to assess the impact of different scenarios on a company's financial performance. Power Query can expedite the data preparation process, allowing you to evaluate multiple scenarios swiftly. Here's what we'll cover:

- Scenario Data Preparation: Learn how to use Power Query to prepare data for creating and testing different scenarios, whether it's changes in market conditions, economic variables, or operational factors.

- Dynamic Scenario Analysis: We'll demonstrate how to build dynamic scenario models that enable you to assess how changes in key variables can impact financial outcomes. These models provide insights into potential risks and opportunities.

- Monte Carlo Simulations: Power Query can assist in data preparation for Monte Carlo simulations, a powerful technique used in scenario planning. You'll gain an understanding of how to set up Monte Carlo simulations and interpret the results.

Real-World Examples:

To illustrate the application of Power Query in risk analysis and scenario planning, we will work through real-world examples:

1. Stress Testing for Banks: Explore how Power Query can be used to gather historical data, apply stress scenarios, and assess the impact on a bank's capital adequacy.

2. Market Risk Assessment: We will demonstrate how to use Power Query to create a scenario planning model for assessing market risk in a portfolio of investments.

3. Economic Downturn Analysis: Learn how to prepare data for scenario planning to analyze the effects of economic downturns on a company's financial performance.

Elevating Your Financial Decision-Making:

By the end of this chapter, you will possess the knowledge and skills to effectively utilize Power Query in risk analysis and scenario planning. This will empower you to make well-informed financial decisions and navigate the complex landscape of financial analysis with confidence. Get ready to enhance your financial analysis toolkit with Power Query.

Part 20. Power Query for Text and Natural Language Processing

20.1 Text Data Extraction and Analysis

In an increasingly data-driven world, text data has become a valuable source of information for businesses and organizations. Understanding how to efficiently extract, transform, and analyze text data is a skill that can provide invaluable insights. This chapter is dedicated to exploring how Power Query can be a powerful tool for text data extraction and analysis, offering a comprehensive guide to the process.

Powerful Text Data Extraction:

Text data is diverse and can come from various sources, including documents, social media, customer reviews, and more. Power Query excels in handling the acquisition and preparation of this data for analysis. Here's what you'll learn:

- Data Collection: Explore how Power Query can be used to collect text data from a range of sources, such as web scraping, document extraction, or data feeds. We'll provide hands-on examples to illustrate these processes.

- Text Cleaning: Text data often requires cleaning to remove irrelevant characters, formatting, or special characters. Discover how to apply Power Query's capabilities to preprocess text data effectively.

- Text Parsing and Tokenization: Dive into the world of text parsing and tokenization, breaking down text into its constituent parts, such as words or phrases. Learn how to create custom parsing rules and apply them with Power Query.

Analyzing Text Data:

Once text data is collected and prepared, the real value lies in the ability to analyze it effectively. This section will cover various techniques and approaches, including:

- Keyword Analysis: Explore how Power Query can assist in identifying and extracting important keywords from text data. Understand the significance of keyword analysis in topics like content marketing and SEO.

- Topic Modeling: Delve into the world of topic modeling, where Power Query can be applied to extract themes and topics from large sets of text data. Real-world examples will illustrate its relevance.

Case Studies and Practical Examples:

To ensure you grasp the practical application of Power Query in text data extraction and analysis, we'll walk through real-world scenarios:

1. Social Media Sentiment Analysis: Learn how Power Query can be used to gather and analyze social media comments and reviews to gauge sentiment and customer feedback.

2. Textual Content Analytics: Explore how a content creator can employ Power Query to analyze blog posts, articles, or textual content to discover trending topics and keywords.

3. Document Processing: Understand how Power Query can streamline the extraction of information from documents and reports, potentially saving countless hours in data entry and analysis.

By the end of this chapter, you'll have a firm grasp of how to leverage Power Query for text data extraction and analysis. You'll be equipped to dive into the world of unstructured data, unlocking its potential to drive insights and decisions for your organization. Prepare to embark on a journey into the realm of text and natural language processing with the power of Power Query at your side.

20.2 Sentiment Analysis and Text Mining

In today's data-driven world, the ability to understand and derive insights from text data is a valuable asset. Sentiment analysis and text mining are techniques that can provide valuable insights into how people feel about products, services, or topics. This chapter delves into how Power Query can be a powerful tool for sentiment analysis and text mining, offering readers a comprehensive understanding of these processes.

Sentiment Analysis:

Sentiment analysis, also known as opinion mining, is the process of determining the sentiment or emotional tone behind a piece of text, whether it's positive, negative, or neutral. In this section, we explore how Power Query can be used for sentiment analysis:

- Data Collection: Learn how to collect text data from various sources, such as social media posts, product reviews, or surveys, and prepare it for sentiment analysis.

- Text Preprocessing: Discover how to clean and preprocess text data to remove noise and irrelevant information, improving the accuracy of sentiment analysis.

- Sentiment Classification: Dive into the world of sentiment classification, where we use Power Query to classify text data into positive, negative, or neutral sentiment categories. Real-world examples and case studies will illustrate the process.

Text Mining:

Text mining is the process of extracting valuable information, patterns, and knowledge from unstructured text data. Here's what this section covers:

- Keyword Extraction: Explore how to use Power Query to extract relevant keywords and phrases from text data. We will provide practical examples to show how these keywords can be utilized for various purposes.

- Topic Identification: Delve into the world of topic identification, where Power Query helps in uncovering themes and topics within large sets of text data. We'll demonstrate its relevance through real-world examples.

Sentiment Analysis Case Studies:

To help you apply sentiment analysis in real-world scenarios, we'll walk through practical examples:

1. Product Review Sentiment: Learn how to use Power Query to analyze product reviews from e-commerce websites, enabling businesses to gauge customer sentiment and make data-driven decisions.

2. Social Media Sentiment: Explore how Power Query can be employed to gather and analyze social media posts to understand public sentiment regarding trending topics, brands, or events.

3. Customer Feedback Analysis: Understand how Power Query can process customer feedback surveys, providing organizations with insights into customer satisfaction, areas of improvement, and more.

Text Mining Case Studies:

To illustrate the application of text mining, we'll provide the following case studies:

1. Content Tagging and Classification: Learn how Power Query can assist content creators in tagging and categorizing large volumes of textual content, improving content organization and discoverability.

2. Trend Analysis: Explore how Power Query can uncover trends and emerging topics within large sets of text data, helping businesses stay ahead of industry developments.

By the end of this chapter, you'll have a clear understanding of how to leverage Power Query for sentiment analysis and text mining. You'll be well-equipped to uncover insights hidden within text data, whether it's understanding customer sentiment, analyzing feedback, or tracking emerging trends. Dive into the world of sentiment analysis and text mining with the powerful capabilities of Power Query at your disposal.

20.3 Language Processing with Power Query

The ability to process and analyze human languages is a remarkable feat, and in today's data-driven world, leveraging natural language processing (NLP) with Power Query opens up a world of opportunities. In this section, we will explore how Power Query can be harnessed for various language processing tasks, enhancing your data transformation and analysis capabilities.

Text Tokenization:

- Text Segmentation: Learn how Power Query can segment text data into words, phrases, or sentences, allowing for more granular analysis.

- Stop Word Removal: Understand the importance of removing stop words and how Power Query can assist in enhancing the quality of text data.

Language Identification:

- Language Detection: Discover how Power Query can determine the language of text data, enabling language-specific analysis and categorization.

Translation and Localization:

- Text Translation: Explore how Power Query can be employed to translate text from one language to another, making data more accessible to global audiences and facilitating cross-lingual analysis.

- Content Localization: Understand how Power Query can help localize content for different regions and cultures, ensuring that data is contextually relevant and culturally sensitive.

Named Entity Recognition:

- Entity Extraction: Delve into how Power Query can identify and extract named entities, such as names of people, places, organizations, and more, from text data.

- Entity Categorization: Learn how to categorize and classify named entities into predefined categories for structured analysis.

Language Processing Use Cases:

To illustrate the practical application of language processing with Power Query, we'll provide case studies:

1. Multilingual Content Analysis: Explore how a global marketing company uses Power Query for multilingual content analysis to understand customer sentiments and preferences across regions.

2. Translation and Localization for E-commerce: Learn how a multinational e-commerce platform employs Power Query for translation and content localization to improve user experience and boost sales.

3. Named Entity Recognition in News Analysis: Understand how a news agency utilizes Power Query's named entity recognition capabilities to analyze and categorize news articles more efficiently.

CHAPTER VIII
Conclusion and Beyond

Part 22. Mastering Power Query: Tips and Resources

22.1 Additional Learning Resources

Congratulations on your journey through "Power Query for Power BI and Excel: Transform and Shape Data." To further enhance your expertise and understanding of Power Query, we've compiled a comprehensive list of additional learning resources to help you sharpen your skills and stay up-to-date with the latest developments. These resources encompass various formats, including books, online courses, video tutorials, and more.

1. Online Courses:

- edX: Explore online courses on Power Query offered by edX, providing in-depth knowledge and hands-on experience. Courses cover topics from basic data transformation to advanced techniques.

- LinkedIn Learning: Access a range of Power Query courses on LinkedIn Learning. These courses are led by industry experts and designed to cater to different skill levels.

2. Books:

- "M is for Data Monkey" by Ken Puls and Miguel Escobar: This book dives deep into Power Query and M formula language. It's a valuable resource for mastering data transformation.

- "Collect, Combine, and Transform Data Using Power Query in Excel and Power BI" by Gil Raviv: A comprehensive guide to Power Query, this book provides a wealth of knowledge for both beginners and advanced users.

3. Community Blogs:

- Power Query Blog: Stay updated with the latest Power Query news, tips, and best practices directly from the Microsoft Power Query team.

- Excelguru Blog: An excellent resource for advanced Power Query techniques, Excelguru's blog offers detailed insights into data transformation.

4. YouTube Tutorials:

- ExcelIsFun: This YouTube channel hosts a vast collection of Power Query tutorials, ranging from basic to advanced topics, and includes practical examples.

- Curbal: A YouTube channel dedicated to Power BI and Power Query tutorials, providing visual and straightforward explanations.

5. Online Forums:

- Microsoft Power Query Community: Join the official Microsoft Power Query community to engage with experts and enthusiasts, ask questions, and share your knowledge.

- Stack Overflow: The Power Query tag on Stack Overflow is a valuable place to find answers to specific questions and learn from real-world problems.

6. Webinars and Conferences:

- PASS Data Community: Participate in webinars and conferences related to data transformation, Power Query, and business intelligence.

- Microsoft Ignite: Attend Microsoft Ignite conferences for the latest updates on Power Query and networking opportunities.

7. GitHub Repositories:

- GitHub Power Query Documentation: Explore the official GitHub repository for Power Query documentation, which includes code samples and insights from the development team.

By utilizing these additional learning resources, you'll expand your knowledge and proficiency in Power Query. Whether you're just starting or seeking advanced techniques, these materials will empower you to harness the full potential of Power Query for data transformation and analysis. Happy learning!

22.2 Staying Updated with Power Query Developments

In the ever-evolving landscape of data transformation and analysis, staying current with the latest developments in Power Query is essential for maximizing your capabilities. Power Query undergoes regular updates and enhancements to provide users with improved functionality, bug fixes, and new features. Here, we'll explore the strategies and resources to help you keep up with these developments and ensure that you are leveraging the most recent tools and techniques for your data transformation needs.

1. Official Microsoft Power Query Blog:

One of the most reliable sources for staying updated on Power Query is the official Microsoft Power Query blog. The blog is maintained by the Microsoft Power Query development team and provides detailed insights into new features, updates, and best practices. Regularly check for new posts, which often include release notes and examples illustrating the use of the latest features.

2. Microsoft Office Updates:

As a Power Query user, you'll want to ensure that your Microsoft Office Suite is up to date. Microsoft often includes Power Query updates in its regular Office updates. Make sure to configure your Office software to automatically download and install updates. This way, you'll receive the latest Power Query features as they become available.

3. Online Communities and Forums:

Engaging with online Power Query communities and forums is a great way to tap into the collective knowledge of experts and fellow users. Some popular online platforms for discussions and updates include:

- Microsoft Power Query Community: Join the official Microsoft Power Query community to connect with experts and enthusiasts, ask questions, and share your knowledge. Microsoft team members are often active on these forums, providing valuable insights and answering questions.

- Power BI Community: Although focused on Power BI, this community also covers Power Query, as the two are closely intertwined. Users often share their experiences, insights, and information about updates.

4. Social Media:

Follow Power Query-related accounts and hashtags on social media platforms like Twitter and LinkedIn. Many experts and users share insights, updates, and news related to Power Query through these channels. You can also join Power Query-related LinkedIn groups to engage in discussions and receive updates.

5. Webinars and Conferences:

Stay informed about Power Query developments by participating in webinars, conferences, and workshops related to data transformation and business intelligence. Organizations like PASS Data Community and Microsoft often host events where developers and experts discuss the latest updates and advancements in Power Query.

6. GitHub Repositories:

If you're interested in the technical aspects of Power Query, consider following official GitHub repositories. These repositories often contain code samples, bug reports, and discussions about ongoing development. They can provide valuable insights into the inner workings of Power Query.

By proactively engaging with these resources and communities, you'll be well-equipped to stay updated with the latest developments in Power Query. Whether it's new functions, enhancements to the user interface, or improved performance, staying informed will help you harness the full power of this tool for your data transformation and analysis needs.

22.3 Power Query Community and Forums

As you embark on your journey to master Power Query, it's crucial to connect with a vibrant community of fellow users and experts who share your passion for data transformation and analysis. Power Query communities and forums provide invaluable resources for learning, troubleshooting, and engaging in discussions. In this section, we'll delve into various Power

Query communities and forums where you can seek help, share your experiences, and stay updated with the latest trends in Power Query.

1. Microsoft Power Query Community:

The official Microsoft Power Query community is your primary destination for all things Power Query. Here, you can:

- Ask Questions: If you encounter challenges or have questions about using Power Query, this community offers a welcoming space to seek solutions. Experienced users and even Microsoft team members often respond to queries.

- Share Knowledge: If you've acquired expertise in a particular aspect of Power Query, consider sharing your insights with the community. Contributing your knowledge not only helps others but also solidifies your own understanding.

- Stay Updated: The Microsoft team frequently shares announcements, updates, and insights into the development of Power Query. Keeping an eye on these updates can enhance your understanding of the tool's capabilities.

2. Power BI Community:

While primarily focused on Power BI, this community also caters to Power Query enthusiasts, as Power Query plays a significant role in Power BI's data transformation process. Here, you can:

- Engage in Discussions: Participate in discussions related to Power Query and Power BI. Users often share their experiences and solutions, creating a vibrant learning environment.

- Explore User Stories: Learn from real-world examples by reading about how others have used Power Query to solve specific data challenges.

- Stay Informed: Keep an eye out for Power Query-related updates and announcements. Many community members share information about new features and functionalities.

3. Stack Overflow:

Stack Overflow is a well-known platform for technical questions and answers. The Power Query tag on Stack Overflow is a great place to ask specific technical questions and receive detailed responses from the broader development community.

4. LinkedIn Groups:

On LinkedIn, you can find various groups dedicated to Power Query and data transformation. These groups often host discussions, webinars, and share informative articles. Joining them can be a valuable addition to your professional network.

5. Twitter and Social Media:

Follow Power Query-related accounts and hashtags on platforms like Twitter and LinkedIn. Many experts and enthusiasts share insights, updates, and news related to Power Query developments. Engaging in conversations on social media is another way to stay connected with the community.

6. Local User Groups and Meetups:

Depending on your location, you might find local user groups or meetups focused on Power Query. These in-person or virtual gatherings are excellent opportunities to network, learn, and share your experiences with like-minded individuals.

By actively participating in these Power Query communities and forums, you can tap into a wealth of knowledge, seek assistance when needed, and stay up-to-date with the latest trends and developments in the world of data transformation. Your engagement with the community will not only enhance your skills but also enrich the collective knowledge of Power Query users worldwide.

Appendices

Appendix A: Power Query Function Reference

The Power Query function reference serves as a comprehensive and detailed guide to the multitude of functions available within Power Query. In this appendix, we provide an extensive list of functions, along with explanations and practical examples to help you harness the full potential of Power Query for transforming and shaping your data.

1. Text Functions:

- Text.Length: This function returns the number of characters in a text string. For example, to count the characters in the "Hello, World!" string, use `Text.Length("Hello, World!")`, which would return `13`.

- Text.Upper: To convert a text string to uppercase, use `Text.Upper("example")`, which would result in "EXAMPLE".

- Text.Lower: Conversely, you can convert a text string to lowercase with `Text.Lower("EXAMPLE")`, yielding "example".

2. Number Functions:

- Number.FromText: This function allows you to convert a text string into a number. For example, `Number.FromText("42")` would return the numeric value `42`.

- Number.Round: To round a number to a specific number of decimal places, use `Number.Round(3.14159, 2)`, which results in `3.14`.

- Number.Power: This function raises a number to a specified power. For instance, `Number.Power(2, 3)` returns `8`.

3. Date and Time Functions:

- Date.Year: To extract the year from a date, use `Date.Year(#date(2023, 11, 8))`, which returns `2023`.

- Date.AddDays: You can add a specific number of days to a date with this function. For example, `Date.AddDays(#date(2023, 11, 8), 7)` would result in a date 7 days later.

- Time.Hour: To extract the hour from a time value, use `Time.Hour(#time(13, 45, 0))`, which returns `13`.

4. List Functions:

- List.FirstN: This function allows you to extract the first N items from a list. For example, `List.FirstN({1, 2, 3, 4, 5}, 3)` would return `{1, 2, 3}`.

- List.Transform: To apply a function to each item in a list, you can use `List.Transform`. For instance, `List.Transform({1, 2, 3}, each _ * 2)` would yield `{2, 4, 6}`.

- List.Sort: You can sort a list in ascending or descending order using `List.Sort`. For example, `List.Sort({3, 1, 4, 1, 5}, Order.Ascending)` would result in `{1, 1, 3, 4, 5}`.

5. Table Functions:

- Table.SelectColumns: To select specific columns from a table, you can use `Table.SelectColumns`. For instance, `Table.SelectColumns(Source, {"Column1", "Column2"})` would return a new table with only the specified columns.

- Table.AddColumn: This function allows you to add a new column to a table. For example, `Table.AddColumn(Source, "NewColumn", each [Column1] + [Column2])` would create a new column "NewColumn" with the sum of "Column1" and "Column2".

- Table.Group: You can group rows in a table based on a specific column using `Table.Group`. For instance, `Table.Group(Source, "Category", {{"TotalSales", each List.Sum([Sales]), type number}})` groups the data by the "Category" column and calculates the total sales for each category.

This is just a small sample of the Power Query functions covered in the appendix. Each function is accompanied by detailed explanations and practical examples to ensure you have a solid grasp of how to use them effectively in your data transformation and analysis endeavors. The Power Query Function Reference serves as an indispensable resource for both beginners and experienced users, making your data transformation tasks more efficient and powerful.

Appendix B: Troubleshooting Common Issues

In this comprehensive appendix, we address common issues and challenges that Power Query users might encounter during their data transformation and shaping journey. Troubleshooting is an essential skill to master, as it allows you to navigate and overcome roadblocks effectively. This section provides detailed guidance, specific scenarios, and practical solutions to common problems.

1. Data Source Connection Problems:

- Issue 1: Connection Failures to External Data Source

 Symptom: You're unable to connect to an external data source, and you receive error messages.

 Resolution: We guide you through troubleshooting connectivity issues, including checking credentials, verifying network settings, and dealing with firewall restrictions. We'll provide step-by-step solutions and practical examples to help you resolve connection problems effectively.

2. Data Transformation Challenges:

- Issue 2: Handling Missing or Inconsistent Data

 Symptom: Your data contains missing values, and you're not sure how to handle them.

Resolution: We'll show you techniques to deal with missing data, including using the "Fill Down" approach and conditional column creation.

- Issue 3: Managing Data Type Mismatches

Symptom: Power Query is recognizing data types incorrectly or encountering issues with data type conversions.

Resolution: Learn how to resolve data type conflicts, including custom data type definitions and casting examples.

3. Performance Optimization:

- Issue 4: Slow Data Refresh and Query Performance

Symptom: Your queries are running slowly or causing system performance issues.

Resolution: We provide tips and best practices for optimizing Power Query performance, including query folding, reducing data loads, and query dependencies.

4. Data Cleaning and Transformation Techniques:

- Issue 5: Dealing with Duplicates and Duplicate Removal

Symptom: Your dataset has duplicate rows, and you want to deduplicate it.

Resolution: Explore methods for identifying and removing duplicate records, including using the "Remove Duplicates" feature and custom duplicate detection.

- Issue 6: Cleaning and Standardizing Text Data

Symptom: Text data is messy and inconsistent.

Resolution: We'll illustrate text cleaning and standardization techniques, such as using Text.Trim, Text.Proper, and Text.Replace functions.

5. Error Handling:

- Issue 7: Managing Errors and Exceptions

Symptom: You encounter errors during data transformation, and you need to handle them effectively.

Resolution: Learn how to set up error handling in Power Query, including error tables, custom error messages, and conditional logic to address exceptions.

6. Advanced Troubleshooting:

- Issue 8: Advanced Topics and Complex Scenarios

Symptom: You're dealing with intricate scenarios or specialized data transformation needs.

Resolution: We delve into advanced topics, such as custom functions, recursive transformations, and merging queries with varying structures.

Each section provides practical examples, step-by-step solutions, and real-world scenarios to guide you through resolving these common issues. This Troubleshooting Common Issues appendix is a valuable resource to help you overcome obstacles in your Power Query journey and achieve more efficient and error-free data transformations.

Appendix C: Frequently Asked Questions (FAQ)

In this appendix, we compile a comprehensive list of frequently asked questions related to Power Query, addressing the common queries and concerns of users. We provide detailed and specific answers to help you navigate through various aspects of Power Query effectively.

1. Basics of Power Query:

- Question 1: What is Power Query, and why is it important?

 Answer: Power Query is a data transformation and preparation tool that allows users to connect, combine, and refine data from various sources for analysis in Power BI and Excel. It's crucial for ensuring data accuracy and consistency.

2. Data Connection and Sources:

- Question 2: How can I connect to different data sources in Power Query?

 Answer: You can connect to various data sources, including databases, spreadsheets, APIs, and web services. Power Query supports a wide range of connectors and options.

- Question 3: What should I do if I encounter connection errors with a specific data source?

 Answer: Troubleshoot connection issues by checking credentials, network settings, and potential firewall restrictions. We recommend reviewing the Troubleshooting Common Issues section for detailed guidance.

3. Data Transformation and Shaping:

- Question 4: How can I handle missing data in Power Query?

Answer: You can handle missing data using techniques like data type conversion, filling down, or conditional column creation. Detailed steps are provided in the Troubleshooting Common Issues section.

- Question 5: What are the best practices for data type conversion in Power Query?

Answer: Best practices include using the "Change Type" option, custom data type definitions, and casting functions. Refer to the Troubleshooting Common Issues section for specifics.

4. Performance Optimization:

- Question 6: My Power Query refresh is slow. How can I optimize query performance?

Answer: You can optimize query performance by implementing best practices such as query folding, reducing data loads, and managing query dependencies. For detailed steps, consult the Troubleshooting Common Issues section.

5. Advanced Data Transformations:

- Question 7: How do I handle duplicate data records in Power Query?

Answer: You can identify and remove duplicate records using the "Remove Duplicates" feature or custom duplicate detection techniques. See the Troubleshooting Common Issues section for a step-by-step guide.

- Question 8: What are the best practices for cleaning and standardizing text data?

Answer: Best practices include using functions like Text.Trim, Text.Proper, and Text.Replace for text data cleaning. The Troubleshooting Common Issues section offers detailed instructions.

6. Error Handling:

- Question 9: How can I manage errors and exceptions in Power Query?

Answer: You can set up error handling in Power Query, including error tables, custom error messages, and conditional logic to address exceptions. Find specific examples in the Troubleshooting Common Issues section.

7. Advanced Topics and Techniques:

- Question 10: Can Power Query handle advanced scenarios like custom functions and recursive transformations?

Answer: Yes, Power Query supports advanced scenarios. You can create custom functions, perform recursive transformations, and merge queries with varying structures. Explore advanced topics in the Troubleshooting Common Issues section.

This Frequently Asked Questions (FAQ) appendix serves as a valuable reference for Power Query users, offering specific answers to common queries and addressing a wide range of topics related to data transformation and shaping. It complements the main content of the book, providing readers with a practical and informative resource.

Conclusion

In conclusion, "Power Query for Power BI and Excel: Transform and Shape Data" has been a journey through the intricate world of data transformation and preparation. We embarked on this endeavor with the goal of empowering readers with the knowledge and skills required to harness the full potential of Power Query, a formidable tool in the realm of data analysis and visualization.

Throughout this book, we've delved into a myriad of topics, from the foundational principles of Power Query to advanced techniques that allow for intricate data manipulation. We've explored how Power Query can enhance decision-making processes by ensuring data accuracy, consistency, and efficiency.

As you reach the end of this book, we'd like to express our heartfelt gratitude to you, our readers. It's your curiosity, dedication, and desire to expand your skills that motivate authors like us to undertake such projects. Your commitment to learning and growth is inspiring, and we hope this book has contributed to your professional development.

We also want to extend our appreciation to the dedicated teams at our publishers who worked tirelessly to bring this book to fruition. Your support and commitment to delivering high-quality educational resources are truly commendable.

Remember, learning is a continuous journey, and we encourage you to keep exploring, experimenting, and applying the knowledge you've gained in your professional endeavors. Data is the cornerstone of informed decision-making, and your ability to master Power Query opens up exciting possibilities in the ever-evolving landscape of data analysis.

We hope this book has been an invaluable resource on your path to becoming a proficient Power Query user. As you move forward in your career, may your data transformations be smooth, your analyses insightful, and your insights game-changing.

Thank you once again for choosing "Power Query for Power BI and Excel: Transform and Shape Data." We wish you continued success and fulfillment in your data-driven pursuits.

Sincerely,